IPHONE 15

PRO & PRO MAX

USER GUIDE

A Complete Tutorial for beginners and seniors To Set Up And Master Apple iPhone 15 Pro And Pro Max With Tips And Trick For iOS

BY

DAVID SMUK

TABLE OF CONTENTS

3

CHAPTER ONE

INTRODUCTION

THE DESIGN

The iPhone 15 models bear resemblance to that of the iPhone 14 models, with the notable distinction being the expansion of the pill-and-hole cutout feature throughout the full range of devices. This implies that all iterations of the iPhone 15 will lack a notch, and instead include the Dynamic Island feature.

The design distinctions between the iPhone 15 and iPhone 15 Plus include the replacement of the Lightning connector with a USB-C connection, as well as the shift from a notch to the implementation of the Dynamic Island. The inclusion of the USB-C connector will be a novel feature across all iterations of the iPhone, while the Dynamic Island functionality made its debut only on the iPhone 14 Pro and iPhone 14 Pro Max.

In addition to the inclusion of the Dynamic Island feature, it is possible that all variants of the iPhone 15 may use an OLED display driver chip built using a 28nm technology. This technological enhancement has the potential to decrease power consumption, hence potentially enhancing overall battery life for these devices.

IPHONE 15 PRO AND PRO MAX DISTINCTIVE DESIGN

All variants of the iPhone 15 will have the USB-C connector, with distinct design modifications limited to the iPhone 15 Pro and Pro Max.

Significant enhancements include the adoption of USB-C connectivity and the incorporation of the Dynamic Island as an alternative to the notch present on the iPhone 14. Additional, design modifications such as an enhanced curvature around the edges and the use of a titanium frame, has been implemented only in the iPhone 15 Pro and Pro Max variants.

UPDATES ON CAMERAS

The next iPhone 15 and iPhone 15 Plus models would have a 48-megapixel camera. This camera technology was first presented by Apple in the iPhone 14 Pro and iPhone 14 Pro Max variants. The use of novel stacked sensor architecture will facilitate the lens in capturing a greater amount of light, hence resulting in enhanced performance of the camera in low-light conditions.

USB-C (THE UNIVERSAL SERIAL BUS TYPE-C)

Apple is switching the Lightning connector on the iPhone 15 devices with a USB-C connection, which will let it to meet with new laws enacted in Europe. The aforementioned restrictions necessitate that Apple manufactures iPhones equipped with USB-C ports specifically for the European market. Consequently, Apple is faced with the choice of either implementing a universal design alteration across all regions or creating distinct iPhone models only for sale in Europe.

PROCESSOR

It is quite probable that both the iPhone 15 and iPhone 15 Pro variants will have the same Qualcomm modem chip, namely the X70 type. The X70 processor developed by Qualcomm presents enhanced artificial intelligence capabilities, resulting in accelerated processing rates, an extended coverage range, higher signal quality, reduced latency, and a potential increase of up to 60 percent in power efficiency.

Wi-Fi 6E

The analysis of Wi-Fi chip schematics provides evidence supporting Apple's transition to Wi-Fi 6E, a technological advancement that will be selectively available just on the iPhone 15 Pro variants. The next iPhone 15 Pro and iPhone 15 Pro Max models are expected to use Wi-Fi 6E technology, although the basic iPhone 15 variants are anticipated to retain Wi-Fi 6 functionality.

In comparison to Wi-Fi 6, Wi-Fi 6E presents a greater bandwidth allocation, resulting in enhanced connection speeds, reduced latency, and expanded capacity. Wi-Fi 6E offers an additional 1.2GHz of spectrum inside the 6GHz band, enabling enhanced capabilities such as comprehensive gigabit coverage for residential environments, multi-gigabit connection for large venues, and increased capacity to accommodate greater data streams required for virtual reality (VR) and augmented reality (AR) experiences.

USB-C DATA TRANSFER SPEED

The next iPhone 15 Pro variants, equipped with USB-C ports, will provide enhanced data transfer rates, surpassing those of the normal iPhone 15 models that will retain USB 2.0 speeds, consistent with the existing Lightning technology. Consequently, the Pro models will possess a competitive advantage in this regard.

The introduction of the iPhone 15 Pro models would provide enhanced transfer rates for various file formats, including videos. The transfer rates of USB 2.0 are capped at 480Mb/s, but USB 3.2 has the capability to accommodate speeds of up to 20Gb/s. If the iPhone 15 Pro models were to have Thunderbolt 3 connectivity, it is anticipated that data transfer rates may potentially reach up to 40 gigabits per second (Gb/s).

CHAPTER TWO

TURN ON AND CONFIGURE YOUR IPHONE

The new iPhone 15 Pro Max can be activated and configured using an internet connection. iPhone can also be configured by using either a desktop or laptop computer. Additionally, you can transfer your data from another iPhone, iPad, or Android device to your newly purchased iPhone.

Note that you can consult an administrator for configuration instructions if the iPhone is being used or managed by a business or other organization.

Get ready for a setup

To ensure a seamless configuration, have these items readily available:

❖ A Wi-Fi network connection
❖ Apple ID and a password; you can create an Apple ID during setup if you don't already have one.
❖ During registration, if you wish to add a card to Apple Pay, do so

To transfer information to a new iPhone, you will need your previous iOS device or an earlier backup of your old one.

Tip: If you do not have sufficient space to back up your gadget, iCloud will provide you with as much free space as you require completing a provisional backup for up to three weeks after you purchase your new iPhone. Navigate to Settings, General, then Move or Reset on the previous device. Tap Start, then adhere to the on-screen instructions.

❖ Android device, if you're moving your Android content

HOW TO ACTIVATE AND CONFIGURE YOUR IPHONE

❖ Hold the opposite button in place till the Apple logo displays.

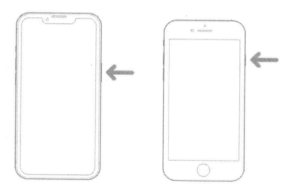

A green arrow pointed to the right-side button on the iPhone.

If the iPhone will not power on, the battery may need to be charged.

❖ Perform one of the subsequent:
  ✓ Tap Manual Setup, then adhere to the on-screen setup instructions.
  ✓ If you're using another iPad, iPhone, or iPod touch with iOS 11, iPadOS 13, or a later version, Quick Start can be used to configure your new device automatically. Follow the on-screen

instructions to securely replicate some of the configurations, choices, and iCloud Keychain. The remainder of your data and content can then be restored to the newly purchased gadget from your iCloud backup.

Alternatively, if both devices have iPadOS 13, iOS 12.4, or a later version, you can wirelessly transfer all of your data from your former phone to the new one. Keep your devices close to one another and powered up until the migration is complete.

A wired connection can also be used to transfer data between your devices

✓ During setup, if you are impaired or have limited vision, you can activate the screen reader or VoiceOver, by triple-clicking on the side icon (iPhone equipped with Face ID) or clicking the Home button (on other iPhone versions). You can also activate Zoom by double-tapping the display with three fingertips.

Switching from an Android to an iPhone

During initial configuration, you can transfer data from your Android device to the newly acquired iPhone using the Move to iOS app.

Note: If you have finished the setup and wish to continue using Move to iOS, you must clear your iPhone and begin from scratch, or manually transfer your data.

- ❖ On your iPhone, perform the steps below:
  - ✓ Follow the installation guide.
  - ✓ On the Applications & Data screen, select Move Android Data.
- ❖ Using the Android device, perform the steps below:
  - ✓ Activate Wi-Fi.
  - ✓ Launch the app Move to iOS.
  - ✓ Follow the instructions on-screen.

HOW TO ACTIVATE THE IPHONE

When not in use, the iPhone turns off the display to conserve battery, locks for security and goes to sleep. iPhone can be swiftly awoken and unlocked when it is time to use it again.

Activate iPhone

To activate the iPhone, perform any of the options below:

- ❖ Press the switch on the side.

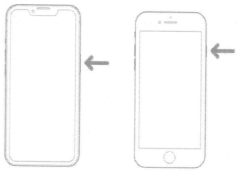

A green arrow pointing to the right-side button on the iPhone

❖ Raise iPhone.

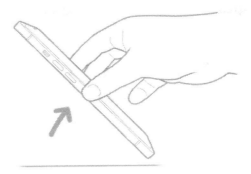

A hand removing an iPhone from a horizontal surface

❖ To deactivate Raise to Wake, select Settings then choose Brightness and Display from the menu bar.

❖ Tap the display (on a compatible iPhone model).

Touch the iPhone's screen to start it up.

iPhone can be unlocked using Face ID

❖ Tap the display or raise the iPhone to bring it up, then gaze at the display.

The lock icon transforms from closed to open to signify an unlocked iPhone.

❖ Scroll up from the screen's bottom.

For relocking an iPhone, press the device's side button subsequently a minute or so of inactivity, the iPhone automatically closes.

Unlock iPhone by entering a passcode

❖ Scroll up through the lower part of the Lock Screen or select the Home button to unlock the device (depending on the iPhone model).
❖ Input the passcode.

To relock an iPhone, hit its side button. The iPhone automatically closes after a minute or so of inactivity.

Dual SIM installation

❖ Navigate to Settings, Cellular, and ensure that you have a minimum of two lines (below SIMs) before proceeding.
❖ Select a line, then select Turn On this Line to activate it.
❖ Select the standard line for data by selecting Cellular Data and then a line. Enable Allow Cellular Data Switching to utilize either line.

   If Data Roaming is enabled and you are outside of the nation or region covered by your carrier's network, you might pay roaming fees.

❖ Select the preset line for voice communications by tapping preset Voice Line, followed by a line.

When utilizing Dual SIM, keep in mind the following:

✓ Wi-Fi Calling must be enabled for a line for that line to receive incoming calls while another line is in use. When you accept a telephone call on one line whereas another is in use and there is no internet connection available, the iPhone utilizes the cellular data of the line in use to receive the call on the other line. There might be a cost. To accept a call from another line, the active line must be authorized for data usage in the Cellular Data preferences (which can be either as the default number or as a non-default line with data access enabled). Permit Cellular Data Switching to be enabled).

✓ If you do not enable Wi-Fi Calling for a line, incoming phone calls on that line are routed directly to voicemail (if accessible from your carrier), and you will not receive missed call notifications.

If you configure conditional call forwarding (if offered by your carrier) from one line to a different one when a line is occupied or out of service, calls do not go to voicemail; ask your carrier for configuration instructions.

✓ If you make a call from a different gadget, like your Mac, by sending it through the iPhone with Dual SIM, the default voice line is used.

✓ If you initiate an SMS/MMS Messages discussion on one line, you cannot transfer it to the other line; you must terminate the conversation and begin a new one on the other line. Additionally, you may pay additional fees if you send SMS/MMS attachments on a line that has not been configured for cellular data.

✓ Personal Hotspots and Instant Hotspots utilize the selected cellular data line.

CONFIGURING CELLULAR SERVICE

For connection to a cellular network, your iPhone requires a SIM card or an eSIM. (Not all options are accessible on every model or in every region.

Setup in an eSIM

Qualified iPhone models can store an eSIM supplied by your carrier digitally. If your carrier supports eSIM Quick Transfer or eSIM Carrier Registration, you may activate your eSIM during setup by turning on your iPhone and following the on-screen instructions.

If the configuration is complete, you can perform one of the options below:

❖ Carrier Activation for eSIM: consult your carrier to start the process of assigning a new eSIM straight to your iPhone. Tap the "Finish Setting Up Cellular" notification when it appears. Alternatively, navigate to Settings, Cellular, and select Setting up Cellular or Add eSIM.

❖ Some carriers support eSIM Quick Transfer, which allows you to transfer a phone number from the previous iPhone to the latest model without contacting them. It is essential to ensure that your Apple ID is logged in on both devices, or that your prior iPhone is unlocked, in close proximity, equipped with Bluetooth functionality, and operating on iOS 16 or a more recent version.

Navigate to Settings, Cellular on your new iPhone, choose Set Up Cellular or Add eSIM, then tap Transfer From Nearby iPhone or select a phone number. Follow the instructions on your previous iPhone to validate the transfer.

When the phone number is transmitted to your new iPhone, it will no longer function on the old iPhone.

❖ Scan a QR Code that your carrier has provided: Navigate to Settings, Cellular, then select Set Up Cellular or Add eSIM, followed by Use QR Code. (You may initially need to select Other Options.) Position the iPhone so the QR code appears within the frame, or manually enter the information. You may be required to input a carrier-issued confirmation code.
❖ Transferring from a different mobile device: If your previous device is not an iPhone, contact your carrier to have the number transferred.
❖ Activate service via the app of a participating carrier: Download the carrier's app from the App Store, and then utilize the application designed to enable the activation of cellular service.

Attach your iPhone to a readily available Wi-Fi or cellular network when prompted. eSIM configuration needs an internet connection.

SIM card installation

You can either obtain a nano-SIM card from your carrier or transfer one from the previous iPhone.

❖ Place a paper clip or SIM expel tool into the SIM tray's small opening, then press the tray toward the iPhone to eject it.

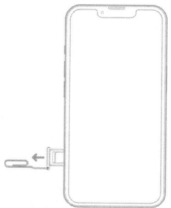

To expel and remove the tray from the iPhone's left side tray, a paper clip or SIM eject tool must be pushed through the tiny opening.

Note: The SIM tray's dimensions and orientation are dependent on the iPhone model as well as the nation or region.

❖ Take the tray out of the iPhone.
❖ Put the SIM card in the receptacle. The orientation is determined by the angle of the apex.

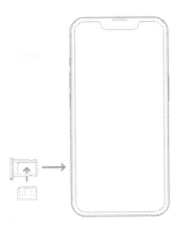

A SIM card is put into the iPhone compartment; the angled corner is located in the upper left.

❖ Replace the container with the iPhone.
❖ If a PIN was previously assigned to the SIM card, enter it when prompted.

Never attempt to predict a SIM PIN. A wrong estimate can permanently disable your SIM, preventing you from making calls or accessing cellular data using your carrier until you obtain a new SIM.

Change a physical SIM to an electronic SIM

You may modify a physical SIM into an eSIM on an approved iPhone model if the provider you use supports the feature.

❖ Navigate to Settings, Cellular, select Setup Cellular or Add eSIM, and then select the phone number alongside a physical SIM card.
❖ Choose Convert to eSIM, then adhere to the instructions on-screen.

CONNECTING IPHONE TO THE WEB

Utilize a Wi-Fi or cellular network to connect your iPhone to the internet.

iPhone must be connected to a Wi-Fi network

❖ Navigate to Settings, Wi-Fi, then enable Wi-Fi.
❖ Select one from the list below:
  ✓ A network: If prompted, enter the password.
  ✓ To join a covert network, input the network's name, its security level, and its password.

iPhone can be linked to a network if the Wi-Fi symbol shows up at the upper part of the display. (To verify, launch Safari and visit a website.) When you revisit the same place, iPhone automatically reconnects.

Join an Individual Hotspot

Sharing a Personal Hotspot with a tablet (Wi-Fi + Wireless) or another iPhone allows you to utilize its cellular internet connection.

❖ Select the device name that is sharing the Personal Hotspot by navigating to Settings, and then choose Wi-Fi.
❖ If prompted, input the password displayed in Settings, Cellular, then hit Personal Hotspot on the device sharing the Personal Hotspot on your iPhone.

Connect the iPhone to a mobile network

If a Wi-Fi network is unavailable, your iPhone automatically connects to the cellular data network provided by your carrier. If the iPhone is not connecting, verify the following:

❖ Check that your SIM card is unlocked and activated.
❖ Go to Cellular in Settings to confirm that Cellular Data is enabled. Tap Cellular Data if you are using Dual SIM, and then confirm the selected line.

When an internet connection is required, the iPhone performs the following steps, in succession, until the connection is established:

✓ Efforts are made to create a connection to the Wi-Fi network that was most recently used and is currently accessible.
✓ Displays a list of available Wi-Fi networks and linked to the one selected.
✓ Connects to the cellular data network of your carrier

On a smartphone that supports 5G, 5G cellular data may be used instead of Wi-Fi. In the event that this is the case, the term "Using 5G Cellular For Internet" is shown under the designation of the Wi-Fi network. To transition back to Wi-Fi, please hit the Information icon adjacent to the internet name, followed by selecting the option "Use Wi-Fi for the Internet."

Please be aware that when WiFi access to the internet is unavailable, apps and services have the capability to transfer data over your cellular network provided by your carrier. It is important to note that this may result in extra charges. Please reach out to your service provider to get information on the charges for your mobile data.

MANAGE IPHONE APPLE ID PREFERENCES

Your Apple ID provides access to Apple services, such as the App Store, iTunes Store, Apple Books, Apple Music, FaceTime, iCloud, and iMessage, among others.

Log in with the Apple ID and follow these steps, if you did not sign in during setup:

❖ Go to Configuration.
❖ Tap Log in to your iOS device.
❖ Type in your Apple credentials.

You can create an Apple ID if you do not already have one.

❖ If you use two-factor authentication to secure your account, input the six-digit authorization code.

If you have forgotten your Apple ID or password, visit the website for Recovering your Apple ID.

Change your Apple Identification Configuration

❖ Go to Configuration > [your name].
❖ Perform any of the subsequent:
   ✓ Upgrade your contact details
   ✓ Modify your passphrase

- ✓ Add or remove Contacts for Account Recovery
- ✓ Manage and view your subscriptions
- ✓ Update your billing address and payment methods
- ✓ Manage Family Sharing

IPHONE SUBSCRIBER TO ICLOUD+

iCloud+ offers everything that iCloud does in addition to premium features such as iCloud Private Relay, Hide My Email, HomeKit Secure Video support, and unlimited storage for your photos, files, and more.

Apple One, which incorporates iCloud+ and other Apple services, is also available for subscription.

Take Note that certain iCloud+ features have system requirements. Depending on the country or region, iCloud+ and its features may or may not be accessible.

Utilize iCloud on an iPhone

iCloud is a cloud storage service that securely saves many types of data, including images, documents, movies, backups, and more. It also facilitates automated synchronization of these files across several devices. In addition to its primary functions, iCloud facilitates the sharing of various digital assets like as notes, calendars, images, folders, and files among others within one's social network. iCloud provides users with a free email account and a storage capacity of 5 GB for their files. iCloud+ offers users the ability to subscribe in order to get expanded storage capacity and other functionalities.

Note that certain iCloud features have system requirements. Depending on the country or region, iCloud and its features may or may not be accessible.

Modify Your iCloud Configuration

Sign in with your Apple ID, then complete the steps below:

❖ To access iCloud, navigate to Settings > [your name] > iCloud.
❖ Perform any of the subsequent:
  ✓ See the status of your iCloud storage.
❖ Enable the desired features, including pictures, iCloud Drive, and iCloud Backup.

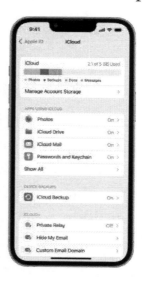

The iCloud settings interface displays the iCloud capacity meter and a list of compatible apps and functions, including Photos and Mail.

28

Methods for Using iCloud On iPhone

iCloud can routinely store your iPhone contents at regular intervals.

Additionally, the following data can be stored in iCloud and synchronized throughout your iPhone as well as other Apple devices:

❖ Pictures and videos;
❖ Data and documents
❖ iCloud Mail
❖ Contacts, Calendars, Reminders, and Notes
❖ Information from third-party compatible applications and games
❖ Messages conversations
❖ Security codes and pay methods.
❖ Safari bookmarks and opened tabs.
❖ Settings for Stocks, News, and Weather
❖ Home and Health records
❖ Voice recordings
❖ Map preferences

Moreover, you can do the following:

❖ Share videos and photographs.
❖ iCloud Drive enables file and folder sharing. Refer to Share iCloud Drive files and folders on iPhone.
❖ Use Find My to find a lost device or to share its location with friends and family.

APPLE IPHONE BATTERY CHARGING

iPhone features an internal, rechargeable lithium-ion battery, which provides the best results for your device at this time. Compared to conventional battery technology, lithium-ion rechargeable batteries are lighter, charge more quickly, last longer, and have a higher power density, resulting in longer battery life.

Concerning Refilling od the Battery

A battery icon with a lightning strike represents a charging battery.

The battery symbol in the upper-right corner indicates the remaining battery life or charging status. When synchronizing or using iPhone, the battery charging will be more prolonged.

If iPhone's battery is extremely low, it might indicate a picture of depleted batteries, indicating that it must be charged more before use. If your iPhone's battery is exceedingly low when you begin charging it, the screen may be blank for up to two minutes before the low-battery icon appears. If your iPod or iPhone touch won't charge.

C battery

For iPhone charging, apply any of the subsequent methods:

❖ Link iPhone to a power receptacle using the included charging cable and a separately sold power adapter.

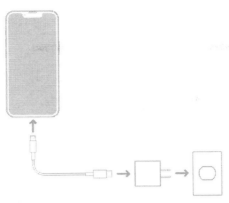

iPhone inserted into a power receptacle via the power adaptor.

❖ Place the iPhone face-up on a MagSafe Charger or MagSafe Duo Charger (connected to an Apple 20W USB-C power adapter or other suitable power adapter) or a Qi-certified charger.

❖ Cable-connect your iPhone to the computer.

Ensure that your computer is on; if the iPhone is attached to a computer that is off, the battery may deplete rather than charge. Check the battery icon for the Charging icon⚡ to determine if your iPhone is powering.

Note: If your keyboard lacks a high-power USB interface, you cannot charge your iPhone by connecting it to your keyboard.

When an iPhone is plugged into an electrical receptacle or placed on a wireless charger, a backup to iCloud or wireless pc sync can be initiated.

Warning: If you fear there may be fluids in the iPhone's charging receptacle, do not insert the charging cable.

Enable Low Power Mode

Low Power Mode is a feature that reduces your iPhone's power consumption when the battery is low. It optimizes efficiency for essential duties such as making and receiving phone calls, receiving and sending emails and text messages, and accessing the internet. The use of Low Power Mode on an iPhone model equipped with ProMotion display technology results in the limitation of the display refresh rate to 60 frames per second. In Low Power Mode, your iPhone might conduct some duties more slowly.

Take Note: If iPhone automatically enters Low Power Mode, it exits Low Power Mode after 80% charging.

To manually activate or deactivate Low Power Mode, use one of the subsequent methods:

❖ Go to Settings, Battery in the Settings menu.
❖ In the Command Center: select Low Power Mode under Settings, Control Center to add it to the Control Center.

Optimize battery charging for the iPhone

The iPhone has a feature that mitigates the procèss of battery degradation by minimizing the duration it remains at full charge. This setting employs machine learning to determine your daily charging pattern, then delays charging beyond 80% until you need the device.

To activate Optimized Battery Charging, select Settings, Battery, Health & Charging from the menu.

Battery lifetime and cycle of charge vary based on usage and configuration. Apple or an Apple-authorized service provider should service or recycle the iPhone's battery.

CHECK THE CONDITION AND UTILIZATION OF THE IPHONE'S BATTERY

You can observe information about the condition of your iPhone's battery and discover how usage influences the battery level.

Review the Battery Status of Your iPhone

Tap Battery Health & Charging in the Settings app then Battery.

iPhone displays information regarding the battery's capacity, optimum performance, and whether it requires maintenance.

View the Battery Consumption Data

Go to Battery under Settings.

Information regarding battery consumption and activity for the past 24 hours as well as the previous 10 days is displayed.

❖ You may find insights regarding the conditions or utilization patterns that cause the iPhone to draw in energy. There may also be recommendations for reducing energy consumption. Tap the suggestion to access the corresponding configuration.

❖ Last Charged: Indicates the last time the battery was fully charged and when it was last disconnected.

❖ Displays the battery level, charging intervals, and times when the iPhone was in Low Power Mode or the battery was extremely low.

❖ Battery Consumption graph (in the Last 10 Days): Displays the daily battery usage percentage.

❖ Displays activity over time, broken down by if the screen had been on or off.

❖ Screen On and Screen Off: Displays the total action for the selected period for when the screen had been on and off. The Last 10 Days view displays the daily average.

❖ Battery Utilization by App: Displays the percentage of battery consumed by each app during the specified period.

❖ Activity by App: Displays the quantity of time spent using each app during the specified time interval.

Note: To view battery data for a particular hour or day, select the desired time interval on the graph. To deselect it, touch the graph's border.

Battery life as well as charge cycles vary based on usage and configuration. Apple or an Apple-authorized service provider should service or recycle the iPhone's battery.

Display the iPhone's Battery Percent

In the status indicator, you can see what percentage of charge remains in your iPhone's battery. Additionally, you can add an application to the Home Screen to track the battery levels of the iPhone and connected gadgets (such as AirPods and additional devices).

Displaying the Battery Percentage in Your Status Bar

Navigate to Settings, Battery, and enable Battery Percentage.

On a smartphone with Face ID, the percentage of remaining battery life is displayed within the battery icon on the status bar.

Tip: On Face ID-equipped iPhone models, you may also swipe down from the upper-right corner to view the power source percentage in Control Center.

Add a Batteries Widget to the Home Screen

❖ By touching and holding the background of the screen until the applications begins to wiggle.
❖ Select the Add Widget icon + at the very top of the display, then navigate down and select the Batteries icon.
❖ Slide left and right across the widgets to see their available sizes.

The various sizes display distinct information.

❖ When the desired dimension is displayed, tap Add Widget, and then click Done.

CHAPTER THREE

THE IPHONE'S BASICS

LEARN FUNDAMENTAL IPHONE MOVEMENTS TO INTERACT WITH THE DEVICE

A few basic gestures are used to control the iPhone and its applications: tap, touch as well as swipe, hold, scroll, and magnify.

Symbol	Gesture
●	**Tap**. Tap an item on the display briefly with one finger. To launch an app, for instance, touch its icon on the Main Screen.
◉	**Feel and grasp**. Tap an item on the display until something occurs. For instance, if you hover over the Home Screen background, the app symbols will begin to vibrate.
↑	**Swipe**. Move one finger rapidly across the screen. Swipe left on the Home Screen, for example, to view additional applications.
↕	**Scroll**. Move one finger without moving across the screen. In Photos, for instance, you can drag a list up or down to see additional items. Swipe to rapidly browse, and tap the screen to halt scrolling.
⤢	**Zoom**. Place two fingertips close together on the screen. Move them closer together to zoom in, or farther apart to zoom out. You can also zoom in and out by double-

	tapping a photo or webpage. To zoom in or out in Maps, double-click, and hold, then drag up or down.

ADJUST THE IPHONE VOLUME

When on the handset or listening to music, movies, or other types of content on an iPhone, you can modify the audio intensity using the device's side controls. Aside from that, the switches regulate the volume of the ringtone, alerts, and other sound effects. Siri can also be used to increase or decrease the volume.

Siri: Say "Turn up the volume" or "Turn down the volume.

The upper left portion of the iPhone's front panel contains the volume up and volume down controls.

Lock the Intensity of the Alarm and Alerts in Settings

❖ Go to Configuration.
❖ Tap Sounds & Haptics (on models that support it) or Sounds (on all other iPhone models).
❖ Deactivate Change with Buttons.

Volume Control in Control Center

You can modify the volume in Control Center when the iPhone is shut or when you are using an app.

To adjust the volume, launch Control Center and then drag down the volume slider🔉.

Silence Messages, Alerts, and Notifications Temporarily

Launch Control Center, and then tap Focus, followed by Do Not Disturb.

Set the iPhone to silence mode

To place the iPhone into silent mode🔕, flip the Ring/Silent switch to the orange position. To exit silent mode, simply flip the switch back.

The topmost portion of the iPhone's front panel displays the Ring/Silent switch to the left of the volume controls.

When the iPhone's silent mode is disabled, all sounds play. When silent mode is enabled, the iPhone does not chime or play alerts or other sounds (though it may still vibrate).

Even when silent mode is enabled, time alarms, audio apps such as Music, and numerous games play sounds via the built-in speaker. In some countries or regions, even when the Ring/Silent switch is set to silent, the sound elements for the Camera, Voice Memos, as well as Emergency Alerts are played.

LEARN GESTURES FOR FACE ID-EQUIPPED IPHONE MODELS

Here is a reference for the gestures used to interface with an iPhone equipped with Face ID.

Gesture	Description
	Return home. Slide toward the bottom of the screen at any time to go back to the Home Screen
	Gain rapid access to controls. Slide down from the upper-right corner to access Control Center; press down control to view additional options. Settings > Control Center is where you can add or remove controls.
	Initiate the App Switcher. Slide toward the bottom margin of the screen, halt in the screen's center, and then elevate your finger. Swipe right to view the open apps, then select the app you wish to use.
	Switch between active applications. Swipe along the screen's bottom margin to rapidly transition between active applications.
	Use Siri. Just say, "Hey Siri." Or, hold the side button down while asking a query or making a request, and then release it.

	Employ Apple Pay. Double-tap the side icon to show the default credit card, then look at your iPhone to authenticate using Face ID.
	Utilize the Accessibility Shortcut. Click the side icon three times.
	Take a screen capture. Press and release simultaneously the side button and volume up button.
	Utilize Emergency SOS (except in India). Hold down the side button and each volume button simultaneously until the sliders appear and the Emergency SOS countdown ends, then release the buttons.
	In India, use the Emergency SOS system. Click the side button three times quickly till the sliders show and the Emergency SOS countdown concludes. If Accessibility Shortcut is enabled, press and hold simultaneously the side button and the volume button of your choice until the sliders show and the Emergency SOS countdown ends, subsequently releasing the buttons.
	Shut off. To turn the device off, concurrently hold down the side button and both volume buttons until the controls show up, then drag the top slider. Alternatively, navigate to

	Settings > General > Shutdown.
	**Force resume**. Hit and release the tone-down switch, and subsequently hold down the side button till the Apple logo is visible.

FIND YOUR PROGRAMS IN THE LIBRARY

Categories such as Creativity, Social, and Entertainment are displayed in the App Library. The most frequently used applications are located near the highest point of the screen and at the top of their respective categories, making them easy to locate and launch.

The iPhone App Library displays the applications organized by category (Photo & Video, Social, etc.).

The applications in App Library are intelligently organized into categories based on how you use them. You can add apps from App Library to the

Home Screen, but you cannot transfer them to a different App Library category.

Find and Launch a Program in App Library

❖ To access App Library, navigate to the Main Screen, then swipe left past all Home Screen pages.
❖ Tap the search bar at the top of your screen, then type the app's name. Or use the up and down arrow keys to navigate the alphabetical list.
❖ To launch an application, tap its icon.

If a category contains several tiny app icons, you may click on them to widen the category and display all of its applications.

Show and Conceal Home Screen Pages

Locate all of your applications in the App Library, you may not require as many app-specific Home Screen pages. You can conceal certain Home Screen pages, bringing the App Library closer to the first Main Screen page. (When you wish to view the concealed pages again, you can choose to display them.)

❖ Press and hold the main screen until the applications start to wiggle.
❖ Tap the dots that appear on the screen's bottom.

Below the thumbnail images of your main screen pages are checkboxes.

❖ To conceal pages, swipe the checkboxes to remove them.

To display concealed pages, touch the checkboxes.

❖ When using an iPhone with Face ID, tap Done; on other iPhone models, touch the Home button.

With the additional Home Screen pages concealed, you can navigate from the Home Screen's initial page to the App Library (and back) with a few steps or two.

Reorganize the Home Screen

If there are multiple Home Screen pages, you can rearrange them. For example, you can place all of your preferred applications on a single Home Screen page and make that page your default.

❖ Press and hold the background of the Home Screen until the applications begin to wiggle.
❖ Tap the dots that appear on the screen's bottom.

Below the thumbnail pictures of the Home Screen pages are checkboxes.

❖ Touch and hold each of the main screen pages, then drag them to a new location.
❖ To complete the action on an iPhone with Face ID, the user should double-tap the "Done" button. On other iPhone models, the user should double-press the Home button.

Modify Where Applications Are Downloaded

You can add newly downloaded applications to the App Library, home screen, or to the App Library only.

❖ Select Settings, then Home Screen from the menu.
❖ Select whether to add fresh apps to both the main screen and App Library, or just the App Library.

Dictation

With Dictation on the iPhone, you may dictate text wherever you would normally compose. You can also combine typing and Dictation; the keyboard remains visible during Dictation, allowing you to effortlessly transition between voice as well as touch entries. For instance, you can touch-select text and replace it with your voice.

On supported devices, Typing requests are processed in multiple languages without an internet connection. If you dictate in the search field, the search provider may receive your dictated text to perform the search.

You may dictate the text of any size when using on-device Dictation. You can explicitly end Dictation, or it will terminate automatically after 30 seconds of silence.

Note: Dictation might not be accessible in all languages, countries, or regions, and its capabilities may vary.

Using Dictation may incur cellular data charges.

Activate Dictation

❖ Select Configuration, General, then Keyboard.

❖ Activate Enable Dictation.

Text Dictation

❖ Tap the area where you wish to insert text to position the insertion point.

❖ Tap the Dictate button🎤 on the on-screen keyboard or in any written area where it appears (such as Messages). Then, please speak.

If you do not see the Dictate key🎤, ensure that Dictation is enabled. Go to Settings > General > Keyboard and enable the Dictation feature.

The iPhone automatically incorporates punctuation as you speak to type text.

Note: To disable automated punctuation, navigate to Settings > General > Keyboard and disable Auto-Punctuation.

You may add emoji by uttering their names (such as "mind-blown emoji" or "happy emoji") as you dictate text.

❖ Tap the end Dictation icon🎤 when done.

Tap to begin dictation.

In the bottom-right area of the on-screen keyboard is the Dictate button, which you can touch to begin dictating text.

iPhone's Onscreen Interface Is Used For Input

In iPhone applications, the onscreen keyboard can be used to input and edit text. You can also input text using Magic Keyboard and Dictation.

Utilize the On-Screen Keyboard to Enter Content

Tap a text field to bring up the onscreen keyboard in any program that supports text editing. Tap each key to write, or use QuickPath to enter a word by swiping from one sound to the next (not available in all languages). To conclude a word, raise your index finger. You can use either method while typing, and can even transition between them mid-sentence. (If the Delete key ⊗ is pressed after scrolling to compose a word, the entire word is deleted.)

Note: As you move to type, you will see alternative suggestions for the word you are currently typing, instead of predictions for your next word.

You may do any or all of the following while inputting text:

❖ To type uppercase letters, tap⇧ or⇧ press the Shift essential then slide to the desired letter.

❖ To activate Caps Lock, press the Shift key ⇧ twice.

❖ Immediately terminate an expression with a dash and a space: Press the Space bar twice.

❖ Touch a misspelled word (red-underlined) to see recommended corrections, and then touch an idea to replace the misspelled word or input the correction.

❖ Enter numeric or punctuation characters: Tap either the Numbers 123 or Symbols key # + =.

❖ Undo the previous edit: Using three fingers, swipe to the left, and then select Erase at the top of the display.

❖ Make a right swipe with all three fingers, then select Redo at the very top of the screen to undo the previous change.

❖ Enter emoji: To access the emoji keyboard, tap the Following Keyboard, Emoji key, ☺ or ⊕ the Following Keyboard key. You may look for an emoji by inputting a word that's frequently spoken — such as "heart" or "smiley face" — in the search field over the emoji keypad, then swiping through the results. To return to the standard keyboard, tap Next Keyboard, Emoji☺, or🌐 Next Keyboard, then ABC in the corner on the left.

A note is being edited in the Notes app, with the emoji keyboard visible and the Search Emoji field at the very top of the keyboard.

Enable Haptic Feedback for the Virtual Keyboard

You can modify the parameters of your keyboard to hear or feel pounding as you type.

❖ Navigate to Preferences > Sounds & Haptics > Keyboard Feedback.
❖ Switch on Sound to hear the tapping as you type, and switch on Haptic to sense it.

Turn the Touchscreen Keyboard into A Trackpad

- ❖ Touch by pressing and holding the Space bar until the keypad turns light gray.
- ❖ Drag the insertion point around the keyboard to relocate it.

Drag around the keyboard to move the insertion point.

Editing a note with a trackpad after the keyboard was transformed into a trackpad. The keyboard is muted to indicate that it is now functioning as a trackpad.

- ❖ To choose the text, hover over the keypad with the nest finger, then move the first finger across the keyboard to modify the selection.

Type Accented Letters and Other Special Characters

Press and hold down the letter, symbol, or number on the keypad that corresponds to the desired character while typing.

To input é, for example, press and hold the e keyboard key, and then slide to select a variant.

A display of an email being written: The keyboard is displayed with alternate accentuated letters that appear when the E key is pressed and held.

Additionally, use any of the options below:

❖ To select Thai numerals on a Thai keyboard, press and hold the corresponding Arabic number.
❖ Tap a suggested letter or candidate at the top of the Japanese, Chinese, or Arabic keypad to input it, or scroll left to see additional candidates.

Take note: to see the entire list of candidates, select the arrow to the right. Tap the downward Arrow to return to the filtered list.

How to Move A Text

In a text-editing application, select the text to be moved.

A note in the Notebook app with a specified phrase within a paragraph

❖ Hold down the highlighted text until it rises, then drag it to a new location within the application.

When you drag to the bottom or the top of a lengthy document, the document scrolls automatically.

Touch and hold the selection until it appears to rise.

A selected phrase within a note in the Notes application appears to ascend when the user touches and holds the selection.

If you decide against relocating the text, elevate your finger before dragging or dragging the text of the display.

How to Set the Keyboard Options

You can enable special iPhone typing features, such as text prediction and auto-correction, to facilitate your input.

❖ Press down the Next Keypad Emoji key😃 or🌐 the Change Keyboard key while composing text with the on-screen keyboard, then tap Keypad Settings. Optionally, you can navigate to Settings, General then Keyboard.

❖ Turn on or off the typing features listed below All Keyboards.

Use Only One Hand to Type

To facilitate one-handed typing, you may shift the keys toward your forefinger.

❖ Press down the Next Emoji Keyboard button😊 or the Switch Keyboard button🌐.
❖ Tap a keyboard configuration option: Choose the Right-Handed Layout icon▶⌨, for instance, to relocate the keyboard to the right part of the display.

Touch the left or right margin of the keyboard to re-center the keyboard.

HOW TO TRIM, SELECT, COPY, AND PASTE TEXT

In iPhone applications, the onscreen keyboard can be used to select and modify text in text fields. You can also dictate text or use an external keyboard.

Select text and edit it

❖ Choose text using any of the subsequent methods:
  ✓ Choose a word: Tap twice with one finger.
  ✓ Choose a paragraph: Tap three times with one finger.
  ✓ Select a text block: Double-click and press the first word, then drag to the enduring word.
❖ After selecting the text to be edited, you can either type or touch the selection to reveal editing options:
  ✓ Cut: Tap Cut or press closed two times with three fingertips.

- ✓ Copy: Tap Copy or press with three fingertips to close.
- ✓ Tap Paste or press open with three fingertips to paste.
- ✓ Choose All: Select the entire document's text.
- ✓ Replace: View recommended substitute text, or have Siri provide suggestions.
- ✓ Format: Format the text selection.
- ✓ Pressing the Forward button
- ✓ Explore more options.

A representative email with a portion of the text highlighted. The options for Cut, Copying, Paste, and Replace are located above the selection. The selection of text is highlighted with two endpoints.

Inserting or Editing Text through Typing

- ❖ You can position the point of insertion where you want to insert or modify text by performing one of the actions that follow:

- ✓ Tap the desired location to add or modify text.
- ✓ Touch then hold down to enlarge the text, then drag the insertion point to the desired location.

A prototype email indicating the location of the insertion point where text will be added or altered. The rest of the text is enlarged to facilitate the placement of the insertion point.

Important: To navigate a lengthy document, hover over the right margin of the page, then drag the scroller to the desired section of text.

- ❖ Enter the text to be inserted.

You may additionally insert text that you have cut or duplicated from another location.

SAVE KEYSTROKES WITH IPHONE TEXT REPLACEMENTS

Create a text replacement that can be used to input a word or phrase with minimal keystrokes. As an illustration, type "omw" to indicate "On my way!" You can add your own, in addition to the one that is already set up.

A note with the text abbreviation OMW typed and the replacement text "On my way!" is suggested below.

Creating Text Replacement

❖ Touch and hold the Next Keyboard, Emoji key😀, or the Switch Keyboard key🌐 while typing in the text writer.

❖ Tap Keyboard Options, followed by Text Replacement.

❖ Tap the Add icon ✛ in the upper-right corner.

❖ Input a phrase in the Phrase field and the desired text shortcut in the Shortcut field.

Have A Term Or Phrase That Should Not Be Corrected?

Tap Text Replacement after navigating to Settings, General then Keyboard.

Tap the Add icon in the upper-right corner, then input your word or phrase in the Phrase field; however, let the Shortcut field be empty.

Create a Replacement Text for Input and Word Pairs

You can construct a text replacement for word-and-input pairs when using specific Chinese or Japanese keyboards. The replacement text is added to the user's dictionary.

There are shortcuts for the following:

❖ Pinyin is the simplified Chinese Romanization
❖ The traditional Chinese characters Pinyin and Zhuyin
❖ Japanese: Romaji and Kana

Utilize iCloud To Maintain Your Dictionary Current Across All Devices

Navigate to Settings, [your name] iCloud and enable iCloud Drive.

Resetting Your Dictionary

❖ Go to Configuration > General > Reset.
❖ Tap Reset Dictionary Keyboard.

All customized words as well as shortcuts are removed, and the default keyboard dictionary is restored.

ADD OR MODIFY IPHONE KEYBOARDS

You can enable or disable typing features such as spell checking, add terminals for writing in multiple languages, and alter the arrangement of your onscreen or wireless keypad.

How to Add or Remove a Language-Specific Keyboard

❖ Select Configuration > General > Keypad.
❖ Tap Keyboards, then one of the subsequent actions:
  ✓ Add a keyboard: Press Add New Keyboard, and then select a keyboard from the list that appears. Iterate to install additional keyboards.
  ✓ Take away a keyboard: Touch Edit, then touch the Delete icon ⊖ adjacent to the keypad you wish to eliminate, tap Delete, and then tap Done.
  ✓ Reorder your keypad list: Tap Edit, drag the Reorganize icon ☰ adjacent to a keypad to a new position, and then tap Done.

Change to A Different Keyboard

❖ Press and hold the subsequent Keyboard, Emoji ☺, or Switch Keyboard 🌐 keys while composing text.

❖ Tap the letter of the keyboard to which you would like to transition.

To swap between keyboards, you can also select the Next Keypad Emoji key 😊 or the swap Keyboard key 🌐. Continue tapping to gain access to additional keyboards.

Additionally, you can alternate between Magic Keyboard and additional keyboards.

Assign a Different Keyboard Layout to a Keyboard

You can use a keyboard layout that does not correspond to the keys on the keypad.

❖ Select Settings, General, Keypad then Keyboards from the menu.
❖ Tap the language icon at the very top of the display, then choose a different configuration from the drop-down menu.

USE THE IPHONE'S LOCK SCREEN TO ACCESS FEATURES

The lock screen displays when the iPhone is turned on or awakened. It displays the current time and date, your latest notifications, a portrait, and any widgets you've added. Based on the lock screen, you can view notifications, launch the Camera and the Control Center to quickly access information from your preferred applications, manage media playback, and more.

The iPhone's Lock Screen displays the current date and time.

Obtain Access to Features and Data via the Lock Screen

Even while iPhone is secured, you can rapidly access helpful functions and data from the Lock Screen. From there, perform any of the actions below:

- ❖ Launch Camera: Swipe left. Press down the camera icon on supported devices, then elevate your finger.
- ❖ Swipe down from the upper-right edge (on an iPhone having Face ID) or swipe up from the bottom margin of the screen (on other models) to access the Control Center.
- ❖ See prior announcements: Swipe from the center upwards.
- ❖ Browse widgets: Swipe right.

❖ Apply the playback settings on the lock screen to play, stop reverse, or fast-forward media that is currently playing on your iPhone.

Display Previews of Notifications When the Screen Is Locked

❖ Navigate to Preferences > Notifications.
❖ Select Show Previews, followed by Always.
❖ Choose how to display notifications on the Locked Screen:
  ✓ Select Count to view the number of notifications.
  ✓ View notifications organized by the app in stacks: Choose Stack.
  ✓ View a list of the notifications: Choose List.

You can adjust the configuration of the Lock Screen notifications by pinching them.

Message views may contain text from Messages, lines from Mail messages, and invitation information from Calendar.

Access and Manage Live Activities from the Lock Screen

You can view Live Activities, such as sporting event developments, order updates, and multimedia playing, on the Lock Screen.

You may utilize the playback settings on your iPhone's Lock Screen to play, pause, resume, and fast-forward when playing music, a movie, or other media.

From the iPhone Lock Screen, you can additionally manage media playback on an external device (like your Apple TV or HomePod).

The Lock Screen displays music controls for a remote device.

Perform fast iPhone operations

On the main screen, in the App Library, in the Control Center, and within applications, you can utilize fast action menus and view previews, among other options.

Quickly access the Main Screen and App Library
Touch and hold an app on the Home Screen or in the App
Library to access its fast actions interface.
The Home Screen became hazy, and the Camera app's fast
actions interface appeared beneath it.

For instance:

❖ Touch and hold down the Camera icon, then select
 Selfie.

❖ Tap and hold the Maps icon, then tap Send My
 Location.

❖ Make contact with Notes before selecting New
 Note.

If you contact and press an app for too long before
selecting a fast action, all of the apps will begin to
vibrate.

View previews and other menus for fast actions.

❖ Hover over an image in Photos to preview it and examine its available options.

❖ Hold down a message in a mailbox to preview its contents and view a menu of options in Mail.

❖ Press and hold an item such as Camera or the luminance control to view its options after launching Control Center.

❖ Make contact with a notification on the Lock Screen to respond to it.

❖ Hold down the space bar while typing to transform the keyboard into a trackpad.

HOW TO USE AIRDROP TO SEND FILES TO ADJACENT DEVICES

AirDrop allows you to wirelessly send videos, photos, locations, websites, and more to nearby gadgets and Mac computers. AirDrop transfers data via Wi-Fi and Bluetooth, both of which must be enabled.

Send a file via AirDrop

❖ Open the item and then select the Share icon⬆, Share, AirDrop***, More options, or another button that displays the sharing options for the app.

❖ Select the AirDrop icon⬤, followed by the AirDrop user with whom you wish to share. AirDrop can also be used to transfer files among your own devices.

To transmit an item using a method other than AirDrop, select the method from the row of sharing options, such as Messages or Mail (options differ by app). You can also use Siri to determine if additional sharing options are available.

AirDrop can be used for safely exchanging app and website credentials with a Mac, iPad, iPhone, or iPod touch.

Permit Other People to Send Stuff to Your iPhone via Airdrop

❖ By launching Control Center, touching and holding the leftmost group of controls, and then tapping the AirDrop icon ⦿.
❖ To select who you wish to get items from, click Everyone or Contacts only for 10 Minutes.

You have the option to approve or deny every request when it arrives.

IPHONE'S CAPTURE AND SCREEN RECORDING CAPABILITIES

You can capture an image of the screen as it appears or a recording of screen actions to share with others or use in documents.

Make a Screen Capture

❖ Perform one of the subsequent:
  ✓ When using an iPhone with Face ID, hold and remove the side button as well as the volume up button simultaneously.

- ✓ While On an iPhone with a Home button, hold until you remove the Home button and side button simultaneously.
- ❖ Tap the screenshot in the lower-left corner, followed by the Done button.
- ❖ Select Save to Photos, Save to Documents, or Delete Screenshot from the menu.

If you select Save to Photos, you can view the screenshot in the Photos app's Screenshots album, or the entire Photos album if iCloud Photos is enabled in Settings > Photos.

PDF-Encode a Full-Page Screenshot

You can capture a full-page, sliding screenshot of a webpage, file, or email that is longer than your iPhone's screen and save it as a PDF.

- ❖ Perform one of the subsequent:
    - ✓ iPhone with Face ID, hold and release the rear control and volume up button simultaneously.
    - ✓ iPhone with a button for Home, hold until you remove the main button and side button simultaneously.
- ❖ Touch the image in the bottom-left corner, then touch Full Page.
- ❖ Perform any of the subsequent:
    - ✓ Save the photograph: Select Save PDF to Files, select a location, and then tap Save.
    - ✓ Share the capture: Tap the Share icon ⬆️, select a sharing method (such as AirDrop, messages,

or Mail), input any additional information requested, and then transmit the PDF.

Create a Screen Capture

On your iPhone, you can make a screen recording and record audio.

❖ Select the Insert Screen Recording icon ⊕ next to Screen Recording from the Settings > Control Center menu.
❖ Launch Control Center, select the Record Screen icon 🔘 and then wait for the three-second timer.
❖ Open Control Center, touch the Select Screen Recording icon ◉ or the red status indicator at the top of the screen and then tap cease to cease recording.

Pick your screen recording from the Photos menu.

CHAPTER FOUR

HOW TO PERSONALISE YOUR IPHONE

MODIFY IPHONE RINGTONES AND VIBRATIONS

Change the audio iPhone gives when you receive a voicemail, call, text, email, alert, or other type of notification by navigating to Settings.

On models that support haptic feedback, you feel a press after performing certain actions, such as touching and holding the Camera symbol on the main screen.

Configure Sound and Vibration Settings

❖ Navigate to Options > Sounds & Haptics.
❖ Drag the handle beneath Ringtone as well as Alert Volume to adjust the volume of all audio.
❖ Select a sound type, such as ringtones or text tones, to establish the tones and vibration rhythms for sounds.
❖ Perform any of the subsequent:
  ✓ Select a tone (scroll down to view them all).
  ✓ Tap Vibration, then select an existing vibration pattern or tap Create New Vibration to generate your own.

You can also modify the noises that the iPhone plays for specific individuals. Navigate to Contacts, touch a contact's name, tap Edit, and then select a ringtone and SMS tone.

Toggle tactile feedback on or off

❖ On compatible devices, navigate to Settings > Sounds & Haptics.

❖ Switch System Haptics on or off.

While System Haptics is disabled, you will not hear or sense incoming calls and notifications.

If you aren't receiving telephone calls and notifications at the expected times, open the Control Center and verify whether or not Do Not Disturb is enabled. Tap the Do Not Disturb icon if 🌙 it is highlighted to disable the feature. (When Do Not Disturb is enabled, the icon 🌙 shows up in the status bar as well.)

Customize the iPhone Lock Screen

You can customize the Lock Screen by selecting a wallpaper, altering the clock design, and placing photo subjects in front of the time, among other options. You can also add elements containing information from your beloved applications, such as today's headlines, the weather, and upcoming calendar events, to your Lock Screen.

You can create multiple Lock Screens and toggle between them. Since each Lock Screen can be associated with a distinct Focus, you can change your Focus by selecting a different Lock Screen.

Face ID (on models with Face ID) or Touch ID (on models with Touch ID) must be configured before a custom Lock Screen can be created.

Create a Fresh Lock Screen

❖ Press and hold the Lock Screen up until the Customize icon appears at the screen's bottom.

If the Customize icon does not appear, hover over the Lock Screen once more, and then input your passcode.

❖ Tap ⊕ the lowest part of the display.

The wallpaper gallery for the Lock Screen appears.

❖ Choose one of the available wallpapers to set it as the Lock Screen.

By deciding the time, you can also alter the font and hue of the clock.

By selecting at the bottom right of some wallpapers ☺, you may change the background hue and select other options.

❖ Tap the Add button, then perform one of the actions that follow:
  ✓ Select whether the wallpaper will be applied to both your Lock Screen and Main Screen: Tap Set as Background Pair.
  ✓ Make additional alterations to the Main Screen: Tap Modify Home Screen. Tap a color to alter the wallpaper's hue, tap the Photo On Rectangle icon 🖼 to use a custom image, or select obscure to obscure the wallpaper to highlight the applications.

Modify the Lock Screen's clock design

On your Lock Screen, you can alter the color and font of the date and time.

❖ Hold down on the lock screen till the Customize icon appears.
❖ Swipe to the desired Lock Screen, select Customize, and then tap the Lock Screen image.
❖ Tap the current time, and then select a font and color.

Modify the Lock Screen image

If you select a photo for the Lock Screen, you can change its position and alter its design, among other options.

❖ In order to adjust the location of your photograph, expand the picture by spreading it out to zoom in, use two fingers to drag the image and move it, and contract the image by pinching it together to zoom out.

❖ Modify the image style: scroll right or left to experiment with various photo designs featuring complimentary color filters and typefaces.

❖ If your photo supports layering, such as one with people, pets, or the sky, tap the More icon ⊙ in the bottom-right corner, then select Depth Effect.

Configure the shuffle interval: when you choose Photo Shuffle, you can view a sample of the photos by tapping the Browse button, and you can configure the shuffle frequency by hitting the More button and deciding on an option below Shuffle Frequency.

You can optionally add an image from your photo library to the main screen and Lock Screen. Choose the picture from the Library in the Photos app, and finally click the Share icon. Choose Apply as Wallpaper, select accomplished, and then choose whether the image will be displayed on the main screen and Lock Screen.

Include widgets

widgets can be added to your Lock Screen to quickly access information.

Widgets on the Lock Screen

A custom Lock Screen displaying a photo of Half Dome in the background and elements for the temperature, the air quality index, AirPods battery level, and fitness rings on top of the photo.

❖ Hover over the Lock Screen till the Customize icon appears at the screen's bottom, then touch Customize.

❖ To add widgets to your Lock Screen, tap the box beneath the time.

Tap to add widgets to your Lock Screen

A customized Lock Screen is currently being developed. The date and time, as well as a button for adding widgets, are designated as modifiable elements.

❖ Touch or drag the desired widgets to add them.

If there is insufficient space for an additional widget, you can select the eliminate Widget icon ⊖ to eliminate an existing widget and create space for a new widget.

Attach a Focus to the Lock Screen

Focus facilitates concentration by reducing distractions. You can configure a Focus to momentarily suppress all notifications or to permit only specified notifications (such as those that pertain to your current assignment). By associating a Focus with your Lock Screen, the parameters for that Focus will be applied when you employ that Lock Screen.

❖ Hold down on the Lock Screen till the Customize icon appears.

❖ To view the Focus options, tap the Close button ⊗ after selecting Focus.

ADJUST THE IPHONE DISPLAY'S LUMINANCE AND HUE

On the iPhone, you can dim or brighten the screen (dimming the screen extends battery life). You can also manually or automatically adjust the screen's luminance and color with Dark Mode, True Tones, and Night Shift.

Manually adjust the screen's luminance

To dim or brighten the screen on your iPhone, do one of the actions that follow:

❖ Launch the Control Panel, and subsequently drag the Brightness slider ☀.

❖ Navigate to Settings > Display & Brightness, then adjust the brightness slider.

Adjust the luminance of the display automatically

Using its built-in ambient light sensor, the iPhone modifies the screen's luminance to the present lighting conditions.

❖ Go to Configuration > Accessibility.
❖ Select Display & Text Size and enable Auto-Brightness.

Toggle the Dark Mode on or off

Somber Mode applies a somber color scheme to the entire iPhone experience, making it ideal for low-light environments. With Dark Mode enabled, you may utilize your iPhone while reading in bed without disturbing your bed partner.

Perform any of the subsequent:

❖ To enable or disable Dark Mode, launch the Control Center, hold down the Brightness button ☀, followed by tap the Appearance button ◐.
❖ Go to Settings > Display and Brightness and select Dark to enable Dark Mode or Light to disable it.

iPhone in Dark Mode's lock scream

Schedule automatic Dark Mode activation and deactivation

In Settings, you can configure Dark Mode to activate instantly at night

❖ Select Settings, then Display and Brightness from the menu.
❖ To enable Automatic, select Options.
❖ Choose either the Sunset to Sunrise or Customized Schedule option.

If you select Custom Schedule, swipe the options to schedule when Dark Mode will activate and deactivate.

If you choose Sunset to Sunrise, your iPhone will use the information from your timer and geolocation to figure out when it is twilight for you.

Set Night Shift

You can manually activate Night Shift, which is useful when you're in a darkened space during the day.

Press and hold the Brightness button☀, and then press the Night Shift button☀ to enable the Night Shift mode.

Schedule automatic Night Shift activation and deactivation

Night adjust can be programmed to shift the display's colors to the softer end of the hue in the evening, making the display easier on the eyes.

❖ To enable Night Shift, navigate to Settings, Display & Brightness then choose Night Shift.
❖ Enable Scheduled.
❖ Drag the slider located below Colour Temp towards the more warm or cooler end of the continuum to adjust the Night Shift color balance.

By selecting From, choose Sundown to Sunset or Custom Schedule.

If you select Custom Schedule, swipe through the choices to schedule the on and off periods for Night Shift.

If you choose Sunset to Sunrise, your iPhone will use the information from your timer and geolocation to figure out when it is twilight for you.

Toggle the True tone on or off

True Tone automatically adjusts the display's color and brightness to reflect the ambient light on supported devices.

Perform any of the subsequent:

❖ To enable or disable True Tone, open Control Center, hold down the Brightness button ☀, and then tap the True Tone button ☼.

❖ Navigate to Settings > Display & Brightness to enable or disable True Tone.

MODIFY THE IPHONE LOCK SCREEN

After creating a custom Lock Screen, you can modify the wallpaper, clock design, photo, and more.

After creating a personalized Lock Screen, you can modify it.

❖ Hold down on the Lock Screen until the Customize icon appears.

❖ Swipe to the desired Lock Screen, and then select the Add New icon ⊕.

❖ Perform any of the subsequent:
  ✓ Select wallpaper: Tap a category option (such as Featured, Suggested Photos, or Photo Shuffle) or an icon at the top of the display

(Photos, People, Photo Shuffle, Emoji, or Weather).

✓ Add widgets: Tap the box beneath the current moment (or the date over time), followed by the widgets you wish to add.

✓ Choose a photo design for a Lock Screen featuring a photograph: Swipe to alter the color filter (such as Vibrant, Deep, Tone, and Vapor), the photo background (Natural, Black & White, Duotone, and so on), and the time font.

✓ Add a layered effect to a photo-based Lock Screen: Tap the More icon⊙ in the lower-right corner, then select Depth Effect (not accessible for all images).

✓ Click Focus close to the bottom of your wallpaper, then select a new Focus from the drop-down menu.

Change the appearance of the time by selecting Customize, touching the time, and then selecting the Custom Color icon⬤.

CHANGE THE IPHONE'S DATE AND TIME

The time and date displayed on the Lock Screen are set immediately based on your location by default. You can adjust them if you wish to alter them, for instance when traveling.

❖ Select Settings, General, Date & Time from the menu.

❖ Activate one of the following:

✓ Automatic: The iPhone obtains the right time over the internet and adjusts it for the time zone you are currently in. In countries or regions where certain networks do not support network time, the iPhone may be unable to automatically ascertain the local time.

ORGANIZE YOUR IPHONE APPLICATIONS INTO FOLDERS

Arrange the applications into folders to make them more accessible on the Home Screen.

Create categories

❖ Press and hold the background of the Home Screen until the applications begin to wiggle.
❖ To establish a folder, simply place one application onto another.
❖ Dragging additional applications into the folder.

The folder can contain multiple pages of applications.

❖ To change the title of the folder, hover over it, then tap Rename, followed by the new name.

If the applications begin to vibrate, touch the background of the Home Screen and attempt again.

❖ Tap completed, and then tap the Main Screen background twice when you are completed.

To eliminate a folder, touch the folder to access it, and then drag all of its applications out. The subdirectory is deleted automatically.

Take Note: Organizing applications on the main screen does not affect how apps are organized in the App Library.

Transfer an application from a file system to the Home Screen

Transferring an application from a folder to the main screen makes it more accessible.

❖ To access the program, go back to the homepage page and locate the folder that contains the desired application. Tap on the folder to initiate the launch of the application.

❖ To initiate the vibration, the user should hold down the keys in the application.

The user's text does not contain any information.

❖ To relocate the application, just use the action of dragging it from its current location inside a folder and placing it on the main screen.

USE AND PERSONALISE THE IPHONE CONTROL CENTRE

The Control Centre on the iPhone gives you easy access to important functions and apps including airplane mode, Do Not Disturb, a torch, volume, and screen brightness

Launch Control Centre

❖ Drag downwards through the upper-right corner of an iPhone with Face ID. To dismiss Control Centre, swipe up from the bottom.

❖ With an iOS device with a Home button, swipe up from the bottom. To quit Control Centre, swipe down or pick the Home icon.

Utilize additional controls

Numerous controls offer supplementary options. To view the options available, contact and hold control. Control Center allows you to do the following, for instance:

❖ Touch and hold the group of controls in the upper-left corner, and then click the AirDrop icon to access the AirDrop options.

❖ Press and hold the camera icon to capture a portrait, photograph, or video.

Touch and hold to
see Camera options.

The screen on the left displays controls for airport mode, cellular data, Wi-Fi, and Bluetooth in the upper-left section. The Camera icon is displayed in the bottom right corner. The screen on the right displays additional options in the Camera fast actions menu: Take Selfie, Take Portrait, Record Video, and Take Selfie Portrait.

Add and arrange control buttons

You can modify the Center by adding additional controls and shortcuts to a variety of applications, including Notes, Calculator, Voice Memos, and others.

❖ Go to Configuration > Control Center.

❖ Tap the Insert menu button ⊕ or the delete icon ⊖ next to the control to add or remove it.

❖ Touch the Reorder icon ≡ afterward to control, and subsequently drag it to a new location to rearrange it.

Withdraw from a Wi-Fi network temporarily

To reconnect, touch the Wi-Fi Switch button 📶 again in Control Center.

To view the connected Wi-Fi network's name, hold down the Wi-Fi Switch icon 📶.

Because Wi-Fi is not switched off when you disengage from a network, AirPlay and AirDrop continue to function, and iPhone automatically joins known networks when you relocate or reactivate the device.

To disable Wi-Fi, navigate to Settings, Wi-Fi. Tap the Wi-Fi Switch icon in Control Center to reactivate Wi-Fi.

Disconnect temporarily from Bluetooth devices

To enable Bluetooth connections, select the Bluetooth Switch icon in Control Center twice.

Because Bluetooth is not disabled when you disengage from a device, location accuracy, and other services remain active. To disable Bluetooth, navigate to Settings > Bluetooth, then disable Bluetooth. Tap the Bluetooth Switch icon in Control Center to reactivate Bluetooth. Choose iPhone settings for travel for information on toggling Bluetooth on or off in Control Center while in airplane mode.

Disable Control Center access in applications

Navigate to Settings, Control Center, and disable Access Within Apps.

OBSERVE AND RESPOND TO ALERTS ON YOUR IPHONE

Notifications allow you to keep track of what's new by informing you of missed calls, rescheduled events, and more. You can customize your notification settings so that you only receive information that is relevant to you.

iPhone displays notifications as they appear, rolling in from the bottom of the screen to reduce distraction unless they are muted using a Focus. You can observe them in an expanded list view, layered view, or tally view on the Lock Screen. To alter the configuration of the notifications on the Lock Screen, pinch them.

Take Note: While using an app, you may be asked how you would like to receive notifications: immediately, not at all, or as a scheduled summary. Changes to this setting can be made in Settings > Notifications.

The Lock Screen displays eight app notifications piled at the bottom.

Find your alerts in the Notification Center

Perform one of the options below to view the notifications you receive in Notification Center:

- Swipe upwards from the screen's center On the Lock Screen
- On other displays, swipe lower from the top-center position. You can then navigate up to view older notifications if any exist.

Scroll up from the bottom with a single finger or touch the Home icon (on an iPhone with a Home button) to close Notification Center.

Respond to message alerts

Many alerts in the Notification Centre as well as on your lock screen are organized by app, making it easier to read and handle them. Notifications from certain applications can also be categorized using the app's internal organization features, such as by topic or thread. The most recent message is displayed atop small layers of grouped notifications.

Perform any of the subsequent:

- To broaden a group of messages so that they can be viewed individually: Tap the team. To dismiss the group, select Show Less.
- To observe a notification and execute fast actions if the app supports them (on compatible devices): Press and hold the alert to dismiss it.
- Tap the notification to access its associated app.

Schedule a synopsis of the notification

You can reduce day-to-day distractions by organizing the notifications to be distributed as a summary; you decide which notifications to include and at what time to receive the summary.

The notification's summary is personalized for you and dynamically prioritized depending on your current activities, with the most important items shown first. The summary is particularly helpful because it enables you to interact with notifications at your convenience. You can take this a step further by filtering notifications while focusing on an activity using Focus.

❖ To enable Scheduled Summary, Go to Settings, Notifications, and then Scheduled Summary.
❖ Choose the applications to feature in your summary.
❖ Set a time limit for the summary. choose Add Summary to obtain an additional summary.
❖ Tap A to Z beneath applications in Summary, and then ensure that the applications you wish to have included in your summary are enabled.

View, decline, clear, and mute alerts

When iPhone notifications appear, perform any of the options below:

❖ Handle a notification received while using a different application: Tap to display, then scroll up to discard.
❖ Scroll left on a notice or collection of alerts to clear them, then pick Clear or Clear All.
❖ Scroll left on a notification or group of messages, tap Options, and then touch an option to suppress

the app's notifications for one hour or 24 hours. This stops them from showing on the Lock Screen, playing an audio track, illuminating the screen, or displaying a banner.

Swipe left on the message that appears in Notification Center, tap Choices, and then tap Unmute.

❖ Switch off alerts for an application or group of applications: Swipe left on an alert or notification group, then tap Options, followed by Turn Off.
❖ Change how an app shows notifications by swiping left on a notification, tapping Options, and then tapping View Settings.
❖ Clear your Notification Center of all messages: select the Clear Notifications icon ⊗, then select Clear in Notification Center.
❖ Silence all notifications: choose Do Not Disturb.

When you haven't used an app in a while, you may receive a suggestion to disable its notifications.

Display recent alerts

You can enable Notification Center access on the Lock Screen.

❖ Navigate to Settings > Face ID & Passcode (if your iPhone is equipped with Face ID) or Settings > Touch ID & Passcode (for other iPhone models).
❖ Enter your passcode.

❖ Switch on Notification Center (below Enable Access When Locked) by swiping down and tapping the switch.

.

FOCUS ON THE ROAD WITH YOUR IPHONE

Activating Driving Focus helps you maintain concentration on the road. When enabled, text messages and other alerts are muted or restricted. Siri can read your responses so you don't have to peer at your iPhone. Incoming conversations are only permitted when the iPhone is linked to CarPlay or a hands-free accessory.

The Driving Focus is not a replacement for obeying all laws prohibiting distracted driving.

Establish the Driving Emphasis

You can configure the Driving Focus to automatically activate when you are in a moving vehicle. (You can also explicitly activate it in Control Center.)

❖ Select Settings > Focus > Driving, then enable Driving.
❖ Tap Focus Status (beneath Options), and then toggle Share Focus Status.
❖ Tap Auto-Reply, then select who will get an auto-reply when Driving Focus is active:
  ✓ No one
  ✓ Recent
  ✓ Favorites
  ✓ All Contacts

You can customize your auto-reply message by editing it.

Then, press the Back icon ❮ in the upper left corner.

- ❖ Tap While Driving (beneath Turn On Automatically), then choose when to turn on Driving:
  - ✓ Automatically: If your iPhone detects that you may be driving.
  - ✓ When Linked to Car Bluetooth: While your smartphone is connected to the Bluetooth system in your vehicle.
  - ✓ When manually activated in Control Center.
  - ✓ Automatically activated when an iPhone has been linked to CarPlay.

Receive calls, messages, and notifications while traveling.

If you obtain a Driving notification while in a vehicle, but you're not driving (such as when you're a passenger), you may ignore it.

Click I'm Not Driving.

When Driving Focus is activated and you are a passenger in a moving vehicle, you can receive messages, calls, and notifications.

CHAPTER FIVE

HOW TO EMPLOY THE SAFETY FEATURES

UTILIZE YOUR IPHONE TO CONTACT EMERGENCY SERVICES

If cellular service is available, you can use your iPhone to swiftly summon assistance and notify your emergency contacts in the event of an emergency.

If cell service is unavailable and you have an iPhone 15 (of all models) you might be able to reach emergency services through satellite.

Call 911 immediately (in all countries or territories except India).

❖ Hold down the side button as well as either volume button simultaneously until the adjustments appear and the Emergency SOS countdown ends, then free the buttons.

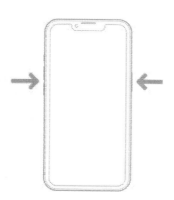

An illustration depicting the volume and Sleep/Wake controls on the iPhone.

Alternatively, you can configure iPhone to launch Emergency SOS when the side button is pressed five times rapidly. Navigate to Settings > Emergency SOS and enable Call with 5 Presses.

If your iPhone's notifications do not deactivate, following an emergency call, the device transmits a text message to the emergency contact list. Your iPhone sends your current location (if available), and those who are nearby are alerted if your position changes for a period that starts after you activate SOS mode.

Call emergency services immediately (India).

❖ Click the side button three times quickly until the adjustments appear and the Emergency SOS countdown concludes.

❖ If Accessibility Shortcut is enabled, press and hold simultaneously the side button as well as either volume button until the adjustments appear and the Emergency SOS countdown ends, then release the buttons.

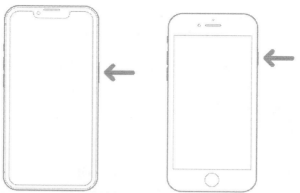

A diagram depicting the locations of the iPhone's side and Sleep/Wake buttons.

By default, the iPhone emits a warning tone, starts a countdown, and then dials 911.

If you do not deactivate, following an emergency call, the device generates a text message to your emergency contacts. Your iPhone broadcasts where you are now (if available), and emergency contacts are alerted anytime your position changes for an extended length of time thereafter activating SOS mode.

If your iPhone is secured, dial the emergency number.

❖ Tap Emergency on the Passcode display.
❖ Tap the Call icon after dialing the emergency contact (such as 911 in the United States).

Texting Emergency Services (not accessible in all nations or regions).

❖ In the To field of the Messages program, enter 911 or your local emergency services number.

- ❖ Type your urgent message.
- ❖ Select the submit icon.

Modify your Emergency SOS configuration

- ❖ Go to Configuration > Emergency SOS.
- ❖ Perform any of the subsequent:
  - ✓ Enable or disable "Call with Hold and Release" Hold and release the side and volume controls to begin the emergency call countdown.
  - ✓ Turn on or off "Call with 5 presses": Five rapid presses of the side button will initiate a countdown for calling emergency services.
  - ✓ Manage your contacts for emergencies: Tap Create Emergency Contacts or Edit Emergency Contacts in the Health section.

Important information regarding iPhone emergency messages

- ❖ Some cellular networks may deny an iPhone emergency call if the iPhone is not active, if the iPhone is not compatible with or set to function on a particular cellular network, or (where applicable) if the iPhone lacks a SIM card or the SIM card is PIN-locked.
- ❖ When you make an emergency call in some countries or locations, urgent service providers may obtain your location information (if it is determinable).
- ❖ Review your carrier's information on emergency calling to comprehend the limitations of Wi-Fi emergency calling.

❖ When an emergency contact terminates with CDMA, the iPhone initiates emergency call mode over a few minutes to enable emergency services to call back. During this time, the transmission of data and text messages is blocked.

  ❖ Following an emergency call, some call features that hinder or delay incoming phone calls may be temporarily deactivated to allow a callback via emergency services.

  ❖ Receiving phone calls (which include calls from emergency services) will be dropped if you do not activate Wi-Fi Calling on a line on a cell phone with Dual SIM on that line goes straight to voicemail (if accessible from your carrier), and you will not receive missed call notifications.

If you configure conditional call forwarding (if offered by your carrier) from one line to a different one when a line is occupied or out of service, calls do not go to voicemail; notify your carrier for configuration instructions.

CREATE AND EXAMINE YOUR MEDICAL ID CARD

A Medical ID offers data such as allergies, illnesses, and emergency contacts that could be useful in an emergency. This information can be displayed on your iPhone and Apple Watch in the event of an emergency and your emergency contact list is notified if you employ Emergency SOS via satellite.

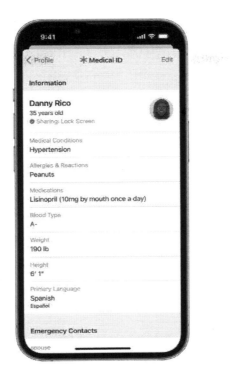

A Medical ID screen containing birth date, medical conditions, medications, and emergency contact information.

Make your Medical ID card

Create a Medical ID in the Health application 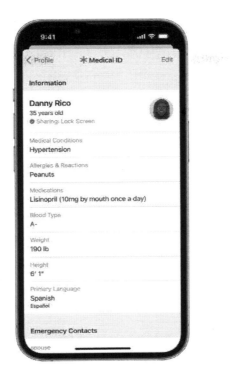.

❖ Launch the Health program on your iOS device.
❖ Select your image in the upper-right corner, then select Medical ID.
❖ Tap Edit or Get Started, then input your information.
❖ Add your contacts by tapping Add Emergency Contact beneath Emergency Contacts.

In the event that deactivation is not initiated, the iPhone will continue to transmit a text message to the designated emergency contacts subsequent to the conclusion of an emergency call. The iPhone has the capability to communicate the user's current location, if accessible, and afterwards, when the SOS mode is activated, the emergency contacts are promptly advised of any subsequent changes in the user's position for a certain duration.

❖ Tap Done.

To access your Medical ID from the Main Screen, hover over the Health app icon, then tap Medical ID.

Permit emergency personnel and services access to your Medical ID.

The data stored in your Medical ID can be automatically shared during an emergency call (only in the United States and Canada) and is also displayed on the lock screen of the iPhone and Apple Watch.

❖ Launch the Health program on your iOS device.
❖ select your image in the upper-right corner, then select Medical ID.
❖ Tap Edit, navigate to the bottom, and then toggle Display When Closed and Emergency Call to the On position.

Medical ID may be accessed by first responders via the Lock Screen of an iPhone by either sliding up or pressing the Home button (based on the iPhone model). Afterward, they can tap on the Emergency option shown on the authorization screen and afterwards choose the Medical ID option.

HOW TO UTILIZE SATELLITE EMERGENCY SOS

The iPhone 15 models include the capability to establish communication with emergency services using satellite technology in situations when cellular and Wi-Fi networks are unavailable. This functionality is made possible through the Emergency SOS feature.

An Emergency SOS display that instructs the user to aim their smartphone at a satellite. It is followed by the notification Opening Messages.

Before disconnecting from cell and Wi-Fi service,

Establish your Medical ID, add emergency numbers, and test out the Emergency SOS demo if you're traveling to a location that may lack cellular and Wi-Fi coverage.

❖ Go to Configuration > Emergency SOS.
❖ Down the page and press Try Sample.

Note that the Emergency SOS demo doesn't start an emergency services call.

Connect your iPhone through satellite to Emergency SOS

If you require emergency services but lack a cellular or wireless internet connection, you may reach Emergency SOS via satellite.

❖ Call 911 or emergency services for assistance. Even if your usual cellular carrier network is unavailable, the iPhone will attempt to route 911 calls through alternative networks, if available.
❖ Tap Emergency Text via Satellite to text emergency services if the call does not go through. You can also text 911 or SOS from the Messages app, then select Emergency Services.
❖ Tap Emergency Report and adhere to the on-screen instructions.

Important: when connecting to a satellite, hold your cell phone normally in your hand; you don't need to elevate your arm to do so or hold it up, but you also shouldn't place it in a pocket or knapsack. If you are surrounded by dense vegetation or other obstructions, you may not be able to communicate with a satellite.

After you're connected, your iPhone initiates a text conversation by sending vital information example the Medical ID and emergency contact details (if you've set them up), your responses to the emergency survey, your location (including altitude), and your iPhone's battery status. You have the option to share the data with those you want to contact in emergencies.

CRASH DETECTION MANAGEMENT FOR IPHONE 15 MODELS

How does Crash Detection work?

If your iPhone 15 detects a serious vehicle accident, it can help you contact emergency services and alert your emergency contacts.

An iPhone screen indicating that an accident has been detected, with the Emergency Call, Medical ID, and Close options displayed below.

The Workings of Crash Detection

If the detects a serious automobile accident, it will show an alarm and, unless you cancel within 20 seconds, will begin an emergency phone call. If you are unresponsive, your iPhone will display a message on audio for emergency services informing them that you have been involved in a severe collision and providing them with your latitude and longitude coordinates as well as an approximate search radius.

Crash Detection will not supersede any existing emergency messages issued by other methods when a collision is detected.

If you are involved in a severe car accident and unresponsive in an area without a cellular or Wi-Fi connection, Emergency SOS will attempt to contact emergency services via satellite, if available.

On or off Crash Detection

By default, Crash Detection is enabled. Settings > Emergency SOS > Call After Severe Crash is where you can disable notifications and automatic emergency contacts from Apple following a severe car accident. If you have enrolled third-party apps to detect device failures, they will still be notified.

CHAPTER SIX

FAMILY SHARING

CONFIGURE FAMILY SHARING ON THE IPHONE

Family Sharing enables you and about five family members to share access to Apple services, buys, and an iCloud storage plan, among other things. You can even assist each other in locating lost devices.

One adult member of the family, the organizer, invites other members to participate. When family members register, Family Sharing is automatically enabled on all devices. The group then determines which features and services to utilize and share.

It is offered on compatible devices.

Five relatives are listed, and the family shares four subscriptions. Create a group for family sharing

You need only configure the Sharing of Families on one device. Then, it becomes accessible on all of your devices using one Apple ID.

❖ Follow the instructions displayed on the screen to configure your group for Family Sharing by navigating to Settings, name then Family Sharing.

❖ Include additional family members. You can designate an adult family member as a parent or guardian when you add them.

Additionally, you can add family members afterward.

❖ Follow the on-screen instructions to configure a feature for the group.

To configure safeguards for a child, touch their name, touch the feature, and then follow the on-screen prompts.

You can view what you're sharing with your family at any time and modify your sharing settings.

What is possible with Family Sharing

Through a group, the following can be created or shared.

* Subscriptions to Apple and the App Store: Apple subscriptions, including iCloud+, and qualified App Store subscriptions may be shared.
* You can share purchases made from the App Store, Apple TV, and Apple Books. All expenditures are charged to the family organizer's credit card, Apple TV, App Store, and Apple Books orders can be shared via Family Sharing on the iPhone.
* If you share where you are with a group, everyone in your family, including those added later, can utilize the Find My app to view your location and locate a lost device.
* The Apple Card and iTunes Cash: You can share an Apple Card with members of the Family Sharing group you belong to or create an Apple Cash Family account to hold a child.
* You may control your children's purchases and how they're using their Apple devices with parental controls

A device for your kid: For an unfamiliar iOS or iPadOS child, you may set parental controls.

Family Checklist can be used to view recommendations and suggestions for shared family features. Tap Family Checklist after navigating to Setting, name then Family Sharing.

JOIN A FAMILY-SHARING GROUP

With Families Sharing, every person in the family uses their ID to join the family group. Thus, you may give access to memberships and other functions without revealing sensitive data such as photographs or documents.

The organizer can invite family members with Apple IDs or establish an Apple ID for a child without one.

Add a relative

A group administrator can add any family member with their own Apple ID.

❖ In the upper-right portion of Settings, [your username] > Family Sharing, tap the Add Member button.
❖ Select Invite Others, then adhere to the instructions on-screen.

The invitation can be sent via AirDrop, Messages, or Mail. If you're close to a family member, you may also choose Invite in Person and request that they input their Apple username and password on the gadget they are using.

Create a child's Apple ID

When a child is too tender to establish an individual Apple ID, the person who organized it, a parent, or an adult can create an Apple ID for him and add them to the group.

❖ Lunch the Settings, [your name] > Sharing with Family.
❖ Perform one of the subsequent:
  ✓ If you are the event planner: Tap the Add Member and Create Child Account buttons.

  Tap Invite Others if your kid currently has an ID. On your device, they can input their Apple ID passcode to accept the request.

  ✓ Select the Add Member icon if you're a parent or legal guardian.

Follow the on-screen instructions to complete the minor account creation. You may establish limitations on content, communication limits, and inactivity; share your child's location with all Family Sharing group members, including later-added members; and use the Ask to Buy feature. These parameters can be modified at any time.

HOW TO CONFIGURE PARENTAL CONTROLS USING FAMILY SHARING

Using Family Sharing, the leader can set up parental controls for the group's offspring. Screen Time allows parents to monitor their children's Apple device usage. The use of the Ask to Buy feature is recommended to enforce the need of parental approval for payments along with free downloads initiated by individuals who are underage.

Modify parental controls during setting

You can personalize controls from the beginning when you add a child to your group for Family Sharing or configure a device for a child. These parameters can be modified at any time.

Follow the preparation instructions on-screen to include any of the ones that follow:

- ❖ Age restrictions for content in applications, novels, television programs, and films.
- ❖ Downtime and restrictions for particular applications
- ❖ Restrictions on your child's communication partners
- ❖ Approvals for purchases and complimentary downloads

REMOVE A FAMILY MEMBER FROM AN IPHONE FAMILY-SHARING GROUP

Family members who are not adolescents with control over their parents or children can withdraw.

Remove an individual from a family

The administrator of a group can terminate members. When an immediate family member is removed, their access to shared memberships and materials purchased by other family members is promptly revoked.

- Launch Settings, [your name] > Sharing with Family.
- Tap [member's name], followed by Remove [member] from Family.

It is not possible to withdraw a kid from the group. You may, however, transfer them to a different group or deactivate their Apple ID.

If you enabled Screen Time for an adolescent, you must deactivate Screen Time before removing him or her from the group.

Leave a category for Family Sharing.

When you exit a group, you immediately lose access to any shared content and cease sharing what you buy and subscriptions with family members.

The organizer is unable to quit the group. If you wish to replace the group's leader, you must terminate the current group and request that another adult start a new one.

- Launch Settings, [user name] > Sharing with Family.
- Tap [your name], and finally click Stop Sharing with Family.

Disband a group for Family Sharing

While the family organizer disables Family Sharing, all relatives are simultaneously removed from the group. Once a Family Sharing unit is terminated, all members will no longer gain access to the shared material and subscriptions.

❖ Navigate to Settings > [your name] > Sharing with Family > [your name].
❖ Select Stop Utilizing Family Sharing.

iPhone allows family members to share their locations and locate forgotten devices.

With Family Sharing, you may disclose your location with other members of the group to assist them in locating misplaced devices. When the family organizer enables location sharing in the Family Sharing settings, the family organizer's location is immediately shared with all family members, including later-added family members. Then, relatives can choose to reveal their location or not.

Inform your family about your whereabouts

When you exchange locations, they can view where you are in Find My. You can also receive notifications when family members' locations change, such as when a minor departs school during school hours.

❖ Select Settings, [user name] then Family Sharing, and then scroll to the bottom and tap Location.
❖ Select the name of an immediate family member whose location you wish to share.

This phase can be repeated for each family member with whom you wish to communicate your location. Every member of your family receives a notification that your location is being shared and has the option to do the same.

You can at any time cease sharing your whereabouts with family members.

Children and adolescents who have Screen Time enabled may be unable to modify their place-sharing settings.

To share your precise location, Location Services must be enabled in Settings > Privacy & Security.

Identify a family member's electronic device.

Once you have shared your precise location with people in the family-sharing group, they will be able to assist you in locating a missing device that has been added to the Find My app.

Your gadgets are at the head of the list, followed by those of your family members.

The Devices section of Find My. The iPhone of Danny is at the very top of the list. The gadgets of Ashley, Dawn, Olivia, and Will are listed below.

ACTIVATE ASK TO PURCHASE FOR A CHILD

When Ask to Buy is enabled, a family coordinator or a guardian or parent in the circle of relatives must approve a child's purchases.

❖ Go to Settings > [your name] > Sharing with Family.
❖ Tap the kid you wish to configure. Request to Purchase for.
❖ Tap Request Purchase, then adhere to the on-screen instructions.

Receive notifications of iPhone usage

When Screen Time is enabled, you can receive a report of your gadget's usage.

A weekly report from Screen Time detailing the total time spent on applications by topic and by app.

❖ Go to Screen Time in Settings.
❖ Tap View All Activity, then perform one of the subsequent actions:

✓ To view an overview of your weekly usage, tap Week.

✓ To view an overview of your daily usage, tap Day.

When a Screen Time weekly report message appears on your screen, you can also access your summary by selecting it. (You can locate the notification in Notification Center if it disappears.) Add a Screen Times widget to the top of your screen to quickly view the Screen Time report.

HOW TO SET A CHILD'S SCREEN TIME

Screen Time enables you to control settings for inactivity, app usage, contacts, and more. Your kid must be employing an eligible device to use Screen Time.

❖ Launch Settings > [user name] > Sharing with Family > Screen Time.
❖ Tap the child for whom you wish to configure Screen Time.
❖ Select Screen Time, then adhere to the instructions on-screen.

Set Screen Time for family members on an iPhone for additional details about Screen Time settings.

You can approve or deny your child's request for more screen time in Settings > Screen Time or in Messages.

CHAPTER SEVEN

THE ACCESSORIES

IPHONE CABLE FOR CHARGING

Your iPhone comes with one of the subsequent cables:

USB-C to Apple Lightning

The Lightning to USB-C Cable

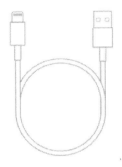

USB to Lightening Cable

The USB to Lightning Cable

iPhone can be connected to a power receptacle using the included cable and an appropriate power adapter (sold separately). You may additionally connect the included USB cable to the USB interface on your computer for charging, file transfer, and other purposes.

Adapters for the iPhone

iPhone can be connected to a power receptacle via its included charging cable and an appropriate power cord (sold separately).

iPhone can be charged using any of the following Apple USB charging adapters. The dimensions and design may vary by country or region.

20W USB-C power adapter for Apple

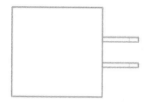

The USB-C 20-watt charger adapter

iPhone 12, iPhone SE (3rd generation), and subsequent variants require a power adapter with a minimum battery life of 20 watts, like the Apple 20W USB power adapter, for rapid charging. If you use a power adapter from a third-party manufacturer, it ought to satisfy these specifications:

❖ 50 to 60 Hz single-phase frequency
❖ Main Voltage: 100 to 240 VAC
❖ Output Voltage/Current: 9 VDC/2.2 A
❖ Minimal Power Output: 20 W
❖ Output Port: USB-C

18W USB-C power adapter for Apple

The Apple USB-C 18-watt charge adapter

5W USB power adapter for Apple

The 5-watt USB power adapter from Apple

iPhone can also be charged using Apple's USB power adapters for iPad and Mac notebooks, as well as third-party power adapters that comply with local and international safety regulations.

MAGSAFE BATTERY CASES AND ADAPTERS

On supported models, MagSafe battery packs and converters attach to the rear of an iPhone or its MagSafe case or cover. The magnets assure proper alignment for rapid wireless charging, and the iPhone can be held and used while charging.

MagSafe adapters can charge other versions of the iPhone and AirPods without magnetic alignment. (Chargers, packs of batteries, cases, and coverings for AirPods and MagSafe are sold separately.)

MAGSAFE CHARGER CAN CHARGE AN IPHONE OR AIRPODS

❖ Connect Use the Apple 20W USB-C power adapter or another compatible power adapter (sold separately) to fuel the MagSafe Charger.

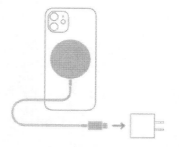

One end of the MagSafe Charger is shown affixed to the rear of the iPhone, while the other end is shown connected to a power adaptor.

❖ Perform one of the subsequent:

  ✓ iPhone: (models supported) Place the MagSafe Adapter on the rear of the iPhone, its MagSafe case, or its MagSafe sleeve. When an iPhone is charging, the charging symbol appears.

  Remove the iPhone Leather Wallet before attaching the MagSafe Charger to the rear of the iPhone.

  ✓ Additional iPhone models: Place the iPhone face-up in the middle of the MagSafe Charger. The power source Charging symbol shows up in the status bar when the iPhone is aligned correctly with the charger.

  ✓ AirPods (2nd Gen) with a Wireless Charging Case in AirPods (3rd Gen) and AirPods Pro: Place your AirPods in the charging container, close the lid, and then place the charging case with the status indicator facing up in the center of the MagSafe Charger. When the case is appropriately aligned towards the charger, its status light illuminates for a few seconds and subsequently turns off while charging continues.

CHARGING IPHONE VIA MAGSAFE BATTERY PACK

MagSafe Battery Pack attaches magnetically to compatible models and extends battery life.

Remove the iPhone Leather Wallet before installing the MagSafe Battery Pack.

❖ **iPhone charging on the go**: The MagSafe Battery Pack may be affixed to the back of the iPhone, its MagSafe case, or its MagSafe sleeve. When an iPhone is connected to a power source and during the process of charging, the device displays a charging symbol.

❖ **Check your iPhone battery condition and MagSafe Battery Pack**: Check the Batteries icon on the Today view or Home screen.

❖ To charge the iPhone and connect it to the MagSafe Battery Pack, use the USB-C to Lightning connection together with the Apple 20W USB-C power adapter or another power converter that is suitable (with a minimum power output of 20 volts). Please note that the MagSafe Battery Pack has to be separately purchased. When the MagSafe Battery Pack is being charged, its status indicator emits an amber light. Once the charging process is over, the status indicator changes to green.

Note: Charging is limited to 90 percent by default to maximize the battery's lifespan. To change the charging limit, launch Control Center, select Low Power Mode, and then select Charge past 90%.

MagSafe Battery Pack may also be charged without iPhone.

QI-CERTIFIED INDUCTIVE IPHONE ADAPTERS

iPhone can be charged wirelessly with a Qi-certified adapter (sold separately). You can also power AirPods with a Qi-certified adaptor.

Qi-certified adaptor for charging iPhone or AirPods

❖ Connect the adaptor to the power source. Use the power adapter that came with your charger or one that the manufacturer recommends.
❖ Perform one of the subsequent:
   ✓ iPhone: Place the iPhone face up on the charger's center. The Battery Charging icon appears in the status bar when the iPhone is aligned correctly with the charger.
   ✓ To charge the AirPods (2nd Generation) with a Wireless Charging Case, AirPods (3rd Generation), and AirPods Pro, it is recommended to place the AirPods in the case, seal the lid, and then set the case in the centre of the charger with the charging status light pointing upwards. When the case is correctly positioned in relation to the battery charger, the indicator light will briefly glow and then

switch off, indicating that the charging process is ongoing.

AIRPODS ARE COMPATIBLE WITH IPHONE

Once the process of connecting the Earbuds to the iPhone is completed, the AirPods may be used for the purpose of listening to audio that is being played on the iPhone. Additionally, they can be used to listen to and reply to messages, send and receive phone calls, and get timely reminders, among other functionalities.

Linking AirPods to iPhone

❖ Launch Settings > Bluetooth on your iPhone to enable Bluetooth.
❖ Navigate to the iPhone's Home screen.
❖ Perform one of the subsequent:
  ✓ First, second, and third-generation AirPods and AirPods Pro: Open the case containing your AirPods and place it next to your iPhone.
  ✓ AirPods Max: Remove the AirPods Max from the Smart Case and place them next to your iPhone.
❖ Follow the instructions on-screen, then tap Done.

Note: If synchronization instructions do not appear on-screen, navigate to Settings > Bluetooth and pick your AirPods Max. If the AirPods Max status indicator is not flashing white, hold down the noise control button until it does.

Utilize earpods with an iPhone

iPhone users can use EarPods to listen to music, watch videos, and make phone conversations. The EarPods are equipped with a microphone, volume controls, and a center button.

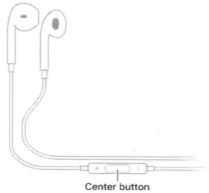

Center button

Even when iPhone is locked, the center button can be used to answer and terminate calls, control audio and video playback, and activate Siri.

The center switch is located on the cable connecting to the right earpiece on Apple EarPods.

EarPods allow for audio management

❖ Press the center icon to pause. Press again to continue playing.

❖ To advance, rapidly press the center trigger twice.

❖ To advance in reverse, rapidly press the center button three times.

❖ To fast-forward, press and hold the center button twice rapidly.

Handle conversations with the EarPods

❖ To accept a contact, press the center icon.

- ❖ To terminate the active contact, press the center icon.
- ❖ Transfer to an incoming or on-hold call and place the current contact on pause. Select the central icon. Press again to return to the previous call.

Combine Apple Watch and iPhone

Tap the Apple Watch app on your iPhone, then follow the on-screen instructions.

iPhone unlocking with Apple Watch

You can use your Apple Watch (Series 3 and later) to securely activate your iPhone (Face ID models) when you're donning a face mask (watchOS 7.4 or later is required).

To enable Apple Watch for unlocking your iPhone, perform the steps below:

- ❖ Navigate to the Settings, Face ID & Passcode menu.
- ❖ Turn on Apple Watch (below Unlock with Apple Watch) by scrolling down.

If you have multiple watches, you must activate the settings for each one.

To activate your iPhone while wearing your Apple Watch and a face mask, raise or touch your iPhone's screen to alert it, then gaze at it.

Take note: For unlocking your iPhone, your Apple Watch must have a passcode, be on your wrist with the display unlocked, and be close to your iPhone.

Exercise with Apple Fitness+

Apple Fitness+ is a subscription service used in conjunction with the Apple Watch that provides access to a library of exercises guided by expert trainers. During an exercise on your iPhone, in-session metrics such as heart rate and calories expended (which have been recorded by your watch) are displayed. (watchOS 7.2 or later is required; the availability of Apple Fitness+ varies by nation or region.).

Even without an Apple Watch, Fitness on iPhone allows you to view your active calories and steps, set a moving objective, monitor your progress, and view your movement trends over time.

Apple Watch health and wellness data collection

Apple Watch can transmit health and fitness data to iPhone for viewing in Health. Apple Watch can also send alerts to your iPhone regarding elevated heart rates, low heart rates, harsh environmental noises, and more.

PLAY IPHONE AUDIO THROUGH HOMEPOD AND ADDITIONAL WIRELESS SPEAKERS

headphones with Bluetooth and microphones, HomePod, Apple TV, devices with AirPlay 2-enabled smart TVs, and HomePod can all play iPhone audio.

Cast iPhone audio to a wireless device

❖ Open an audio application such as Podcasts or Music on the iPhone, then select an item to play.

❖ Click the Playback Destination icon, then select a destination for playback.

the playback options for a podcast, which include the Playback Destination button.

Note: Ensure that your AirPlay 2-enabled devices are on the same Wi-Fi network if they aren't listed in the list of playback destinations. If you travel out of Bluetooth range with a Bluetooth-enabled device, the iPhone will resume playing audio.

You can also touch the Playback Destination icon on the Lock Screen or in Control Center to select the playback location.

AirPlay 2-enabled devices that can play audio

With AirPlay 2 and the iPhone, you can stream audio to multiple AirPlay 2-capable devices on the same Wi-Fi network. For instance, a party playlist can be played on HomePod loudspeakers in the living area and kitchen, Apple TV in the bedroom, and an AirPlay 2-enabled smart TV in the family room.

Siri: Say a thing like:

- ❖ "Quit playing music everywhere"
- ❖ "Adjust the loudness in the dining room to 10 percent"
- ❖ "What's playing in the kitchen?"
- ❖ "Play a song I like in the kitchen"
- ❖ "Add the living room's speaker"
- ❖ "Remove music from the kitchen"
- ❖ "Move the music into the den"

Additionally, you can select playback locations from the iPhone's display.

- ❖ Select the Playback Destination icon in the Control Center🔘, on your Lock Screen, or the Now Streaming screen of the currently playing app.
- ❖ Select each device that will be utilized.

Stereo devices are regarded as singular audio devices.

Transfer audio from the iPhone to the HomePod

Bring your iPhone near to the top of the HomePod while streaming audio from Music, Podcasts, or another audio app.

These are the requirements for audio handoff:

- ❖ Both devices have to be signed in with an identical Apple ID.
- ❖ You are turning on Wi-Fi and Handoff on your iPhone.
- ❖ iPhone and HomePod have to be within the same HomeKit household and on the same Wi-Fi connection to communicate.
- ❖ Your devices must be within Bluetooth variety of one another (approximately 33 feet or 10 meters) and have Bluetooth enabled.

Launch Settings > General > AirPlay & Handoff to disable Handoff between the iPhone and HomePod or other devices.

CABLE-CONNECT THE IPHONE TO A DISPLAY

Using the right connection or adapter, you may connect your iPhone to a secondary show, such as a computer screen, television, or projector.

❖ Attach the Lightning to Digital AV Adapter or a Lightning to VGA adapter to the charging interface on the iPhone.
❖ Connect an HDMI connection or VGA cable to the adaptor.
❖ Connect an HDMI or VGA cable's other end to the television set's projector, or monitor.
❖ If necessary, transition the monitor, TV, or projector to the appropriate video source.

These adapters have an extra plug for charging your iPhone when it had a connection to a display, TV, or projector.

ENTER CHARACTERS CONTAINING DIACRITICAL MARKS USING MAGIC KEYBOARD

If the Magic Keyboard lacks accents and other punctuation marks for the language you're typing, you can input them using a modifier key or the onscreen keyboard.

Option key is used to add a diacritical mark to a character

To input a letter or number with a diacritical mark, you may choose a mark by pressing the Option key on the Magic Keyboard.

❖ Perform one of the subsequent:
  ✓ Add a language keypad that allows diacritical marks, and then transition to that keyboard in an application.

    Navigate to Preferences > General > Keyboard > Hardware Keyboard to choose a new keyboard layout that supports diacritical markings.

    If you have an English (US) keyboard, for instance, tap English (US), then select U.S. Internacional — PC or ABC — Extended.

❖ In an application, press down on the Option key, then hit a diacritical mark-entering key.

  For instance, these diacritical marks are supported by the Spanish (Mexico) keypad and the U.S. Internacional — PC alternative layout:

  ✓ Sharp accent (such as the example of é): Option-E.
  ✓ Grave emphasis (for example, è): Option-'.
  ✓ Tilde (for instance,): Alternative-N.
  ✓ Umlaut or diaeresis (such as ü): Option-U.
  ✓ Circumflex (such as ê): Option I.

❖ Activate the letter.

To input employing the Spanish (Mexico) keypad or the U.S. Internacional — PC alternate layout, for instance, select Option-N followed by a n.

Note that the alternative layout ABC - Extended also enables you to input tone marks for transcribing Mandarin Chinese in Pinyin. To type in long ("travel"), for instance, select Option-V followed by a v. Additionally, the ABC - Extended configuration enables you to type diacritical marks and characters from a variety of European languages, including Czech, German, French, Hungarian, and Polish.

Enter a diacritical marking using the on-screen keyboard

❖ To display the virtual keyboard, select the Eject button▲ on the Magic Keyboard.
❖ Click and hold the word, quantity, or icon on the on-screen keyboard that corresponds to the desired character.

To input é, for instance, hold down the e key.

❖ Slide along with your finger to select an option.
❖ Press the Eject button▲ on the Magic Keyboard to conceal the on-screen keyboard when you're done.

IPHONE AND MAGIC KEYBOARD ENABLE KEYBOARD SWITCHING

You can alternate among the regional keyboard for your region, an emoji keyboard, different language keyboards that you add, and the keyboard that's displayed using Magic Keyboard.

You can toggle between linguistic keyboards and the on-screen emoji keyboard

❖ On the Magic Keyboard, hold down the Control key.
❖ Press the space bar to toggle among the spoken language keypad for your region, the emoji keys, and any additional language keyboards you have added.

Display or conceal the on-screen keyboard

To display the virtual keyboard, select the Eject button⏏ on the Magic Keyboard. To conceal the on-screen keyboard, choose the Eject button⏏ a second time.

IPHONE USERS MAY COMPOSE TEXT WHILE EMPLOYING MAGIC KEYBOARD

On Magic Keyboard, you're able to dictate text rather than enter it.

Take note: Typing may not be accessible in all languages, countries, or regions, and its capabilities may vary. There may be cellular data fees.

- Launch Settings > General > The keyboard, set Enable Dictation, and then select a shortcut for dictation.
- Tap to position your insertion point, then click the dictation shortcut symbol twice to insert text by dictation.
- To access the Magic Keyboard again, press the dictate shortcut key twice in rapid succession.

The iPhone automatically incorporates punctuation as you speak to type text. You may add emoji by uttering their names, such as "mind-blown emoji" or "happy emoji."

PRINTING VIA IPHONE

Use AirPrint to wirelessly print from Mail, Photos, and Safari to an AirPrint-enabled printer. Numerous App Store applications also support AirPrint.

The iPhone and printer must be connected to the same Wi-Fi network.

Determine the status of a printing task

Launch the App Switcher and select Print Center.

The emblem on the icon indicates the number of documents in the backlog.

To cancel a print task, tap Cancel Printing after selecting it in Print Center.

Print a document

Tap Print after tapping the Share button⬆️, More button***, Reply button↩️, or Actions Menu button ⌄ (depending on the app you're using). (If you do not see Print, swipe up.)

CHAPTER EIGHT

USING IPHONE WITH OTHER DEVICES

HOW TO TRANSFER TASK

Using Handoff, you can begin a task on a single gadget (iPhone, iPad, iPod touch, Mac, or Apple Watch) and then continue it on another device. For instance, you can begin a response to an email on your smartphone and complete it in Mail on your Mac. Handoff is compatible with many Apple applications, including Calendar, Contacts, and Safari. Some third-party applications may be compatible with Handoff.

Before transferring duties between an iPhone and another device, ensure the following:

❖ Both devices are linked to a single Apple ID.
❖ You have enabled Wi-Fi, Bluetooth, and Handoff on your Mac.
❖ You've enabled Wi-Fi, Bluetooth, and Handoff on your iPhone as well as another iOS or iPadOS device.
❖ The Bluetooth range between your devices is approximately 33 feet or 10 meters.
❖ Each device has at least the following software versions installed: iOS 10, iPadOS 13, macOS 10.10, and watchOS 1.0.

Transfer from a different device

❖ Open the iPhone's App Switcher. The Handoff symbol of the app you are using right now on your other device shows at the bottom of the iPhone's screen.

❖ Select the Handoff icon to keep on using the application.

Transferring from the iPhone to another device

Click or touch the Handoff icon on the other device to keep functioning within the app.

On other devices, the Handoff icon for an iPhone app appears in one of the following locations:

❖ Mac: The bottom or right extremity of the Dock, depending on the Dock's position.

❖ The right extremity of the Dock for the iPad.

❖ Bottom of the App Switcher screen on an iPhone or iPod touch.

Deactivate Handoff on your gadget

❖ iPad, iPhone, and iPod touch: Navigate to Settings > General > AirPlay & Handoff menu.

❖ macOS Ventura: Go to the Apple menu > System Preferences, then choose General in the sidebar, then AirDrop & Handoff on the right, and finally stop Enable The Handoff feature across this Mac and your iCloud devices.

❖ macOS 12.5 and earlier: Eliminate "Allow this feature Handoff between this Mac and your iCloud devices" by going to Apple > System Preferences > General and then unchecking the box next to "Allow this feature Handoff between this Mac and your iCloud devices."When Handoff is enabled, you can manually copy and paste text, graphics, photos, and videos throughout devices using Universal Clipboard.

SHARE YOUR IPHONE'S INTERNET CONNECTION

Personal Hotspot allows you to share your iPhone's cellular internet connection with other devices. A personal Hotspot is beneficial when other devices lack access to the internet via a Wi-Fi network.

Personal Hotspot is not supported by all carriers. Possible additional surcharges may apply. The maximum number of devices that can simultaneously connect to your Personal.

iPhone Personal Hotspot Configuration

uses the onscreen direction by navigating to Settings > Cellular > Setup Personal Hotspot.

Note: If you do not see the option to Set Up Personal Hotspot and Cellular Data is enabled in Settings > Cellular, contact your carrier about adding Personal Hotspot to your plan.

You can modify the parameters listed below:

❖ Change the password for your Personal Hotspot's Wi-Fi network: Access Wi-Fi Password by navigating to Settings > Personal Hotspot > Wi-Fi Password.

❖ Disconnect devices and turn off Personal Hotspot: Navigate to Settings > Personal Hotspot and disable Allow Others to Join.

Personal Hotspot utilizes the selected SIM for cellular data if your iPhone is configured to use two SIMs.

Connect a Mac or Windows computer to your Hotspot

A Mac or PC can be connected to your Hotspot using Wi-Fi, a USB cable, or Bluetooth. Perform one of the subsequent:

❖ Connect via Wi-Fi from a Mac: select the Wi-Fi status menu 📶 in the menu bar, then select your iPhone from a list of available networks.

If prompted, input the password displayed under Settings > Private Hotspot on your iPhone.

As long as your Mac is attached to your Hotspot, the Wi-Fi status indicator in the menu area transforms into the Personal Hotspot icon 🔗.

Note: You can link your devices to a personal hot spot without inputting a password when both your Mac and iPhone are signed in using the one Apple ID, Bluetooth, and Wi-Fi are enabled on your iPhone, and Bluetooth and Wi-Fi are enabled on your Mac.

- ❖ Utilize Wi-Fi to connect to a computer: Choose your iPhone in the Wi-Fi settings on your computer, then enter the password displayed in Settings > Personal Hotspot on your iPhone.
- ❖ Connect your iPhone and computer with a USB cable. If you receive the alert Trust this Computer?, select Trust. Choose iPhone in your computer's network preferences, then configure your network settings.
- ❖ To ensure your iPhone is visible via Bluetooth, navigate to Settings > Bluetooth and depart the screen on. On a Mac, link your Mac and iPad via Bluetooth. Tap the address of your Mac on your iPhone, then follow the instructions displayed on your Mac.

Following the manufacturer's instructions, configure a Bluetooth connection to the network on a PC.

Connect your iPod touch, iPad, or additional iPhone to the Personal Hotspot

Navigate to Settings > Wi-Fi on the other device, then select your iPhone from the selection of available networks.

If prompted by the other device for a password, input the password displayed in Settings, Personal Hotspot on the iPhone.

Note: Attach the devices without inputting a password if they share the same Apple ID and Bluetooth and Wi-Fi are enabled on both devices.

When a device is attached to the iPhone, a blue band appears at the top of the screen. The Personal Hotspot icon⌒⊘ appears in the connected device's status bar.

Using Family Sharing, you may share your private internet connection with any family member, either automatically or upon request.

If you share a Personal Hotspot with your iPhone, the internet connection is provided by cellular data. To track your cellular data usage, navigate to Settings > Cellular.

VIDEO AND AUDIO CAN BE WIRELESSLY TRANSFERRED FROM AN IPHONE TO A MAC

You can utilize a nearby Mac to stream videos, photos, and audio from your iPhone. Additionally, you can mirror your iPhone's display to your Mac (macOS 12 or later required).

Configure a Mac to support streaming from an iPhone

❖ Perform any of the following actions on a Mac:
  ✓ Choose Apple > System Settings on macOS Ventura, then select General, AirPlay & Handoff on the right, and set AirPlay Receiver.
  ✓ macOS 12.5 and prior: Choose Apple > System Preferences > Sharing, then select AirPlay Receiver and set it on.
❖ Select one of the options for "Allow AirPlay for:"

- ✓ To restrict streaming to devices using the same Apple ID as the Mac, choose "Current user."
- ✓ To grant access to others, choose "Anyone on the same network" or "Everyone."

To require a password when using AirPlay on a Mac, select the option and input a password in the text field.

If you select "Anyone on the same network" or "Everyone," and someone is signed into their gadget with a different Apple ID compared to on the Mac, an AirPlay request initially needs acceptance on the Mac and verification on another device. Accept the AirPlay request on the Mac. Input the code on the additional device if the computer displays an AirPlay code.

iPhone video can be viewed on a Mac

- ❖ Tap the screen to reveal the controls while playing a video in the Apple TV app . or another supported video app on your iPhone.

- ❖ Tap the AirPlay icon ., then select the Mac as the destination for playback.

A film playing on the iPhone's display. Near the bottom right of the display are the playback controls, which include the AirPlay icon.

To display video playback settings on a Mac, hover the cursor over the currently playing video.

To alter the destination for playback, select an alternate AirPlay option on the iPhone's display.

Display iPhone photographs on a Mac

❖ Select a photo in Photos on your iPhone, then select the Share icon.

❖ Scroll up, choose the AirPlay symbol, and then select the Mac as the destination for playback.

Hit the AirPlay symbol near the very top of the iPhone screen, and then click Turn off AirPlay to cease streaming photos.

Sync your iPhone with a Mac

On a Mac, you're able to observe and listen to anything that is displayed or played on your iPhone.

❖ Launch Control Center on the device you are using on iOS.

❖ Hit the Screen Mirroring ⬚, then choose the Mac as the destination for playback.

To return to your iPhone, launch Control Center, touch the Screen Mirroring icon ⬚, and then touch Stop Mirroring.

Play iPhone audio on a Mac

❖ Open an audio application such as Podcasts 🔘 or Music 🎵 on your iPhone, then select an item to play.

❖ Press the Playback Destination icon 🔘, then select a destination for playback.

You can also press the Playback Destination icon 🔘 on the Lock Screen or in Control Center to select the playback destination.

CHAPTER NINE

COPY, AND PASTE, CUT ARE SUPPORTED BETWEEN THE IPHONE AND OTHER DEVICES

You may utilize Universal Clipboard to trim or copy content (such as a text block or an image) on your iPhone, then place it on your iPad, on another iOS device, or your Mac, and vice versa.

Note: For information on selecting, cutting, copying, and pasting text within and between apps on your iPhone, observe Select, cut, copy, as well as paste text on iPhone.

Ensure the following before beginning:

❖ Both devices are signed in using one Apple ID.
❖ You have enabled Wi-Fi, Bluetooth, and Handoff on your Mac.
❖ You've enabled Wi-Fi, Bluetooth, and Handoff on your iPhone as well as another iOS or iPadOS device.
❖ The Bluetooth range between your devices is approximately 33 feet or 10 meters.
❖ Each device has iOS 10, iPadOS 13, macOS 10.12, or a later version of the relevant software installed.

Copy, cut, or insert

❖ Close the gap using three fingertips.

- ❖ Cut: Pinch three fingertips together twice.
- ❖ Open the paste with three fingertips.

Additionally, you can contact and retain a selection before tapping Cut, Copy, or Paste.

Important: Your content must be sliced, copied, and pasted in a brief amount of time.

ICLOUD WILL AUTOMATICALLY UPDATE YOUR FILES ON YOUR IPHONE AND COMPUTER

Using iCloud, you can save your files, photographs, and videos in the cloud so that they are accessible from any device. The same information appears on your iPhone, Mac (OS X 10.10 or later), and Windows PC (Windows 7). Your Apple ID must be signed in on both your iPhone and your desktop or laptop.

Note that iCloud gives you a complimentary email account along with 5 GB of data storage. iCloud+ can be subscribed to for greater storage space and extra amenities.

Configure iCloud

- ❖ Select Settings > [your name] on your iPhone.

  If [your name] is not displayed, select "Sign in to your [device]," and then input your ID and password.

- ❖ Tap iCloud, then activate the items that will store their information in the cloud.

144

The iCloud settings interface displays the iCloud storage meter and a list of compatible apps and characteristics, including Mail, contacts, and Messages.

Turn on iCloud Drive, for instance, to make your iCloud Drive files accessible on your computer.

Configure iCloud on your Mac

❖ Activate the same settings as you did for your iPhone.

Install iCloud on the Windows computer

❖ Enable the same options that you enabled for iPhone, and then select Apply.

Note that certain iCloud features have system requirements. iCloud may not be accessible in all regions, and its capabilities may vary by region.

CONNECTING THE COMPUTER AND IPHONE VIA CABLE

Utilizing a USB cable or adapters, an iPhone can be connected directly to a Mac or Windows PC.

❖ Ensure that you possess one of the following items:
  ✓ Mac with a USB interface and OS X 10.9 or later Windows 7 or greater on a PC with a USB interface Connect the charging cord on the phone to the USB adapter on your computer. If the cable is unsuitable for your computer's interface, try one of the following:
  ✓ If your computer has a USB-C port, attach the Lightning connector on the other side of the interface to a USB-C to USB Adapter (available separately) or a USB-C connectivity to Lightning Cable (sold separately).
  ✓ If your iPhone came prepared with a USB-C to Lightning Cable but your computer lacks a USB connector, use a Lightning to USB Cable (available separately).
❖ When first connecting the devices, pick Trust when prompted on the iPhone to trust the computer.
❖ Perform any of the subsequent:
  ✓ Initial iPhone configuration.
  ✓ Share the Internet connection on your iPhone with your computer.
  ✓ Apply your computer to delete all iPhone content and settings.
  ✓ You can update your iPhone via your computer.

✓ Transfer or synchronize content among the iPhone and computer.

The iPhone's battery is charged when the device is connected to a computer and the computer is powered.

YOU CAN WIRELESSLY TRANSFER FILES AMONG YOUR IPHONE AND COMPUTER USING EMAIL, MESSAGES, OR AIRDROP

Using messages, email, or AirDrop to wirelessly transmit files between devices is the easiest method to transfer files.

Utilize email for file transmission

Ensure that you've got an email account on your iPhone and computer before proceeding.

❖ Upload a few files to an electronic message and transmit it to yourself using your iPhone or computer.

To transmit a photo from an iPhone using Mail, for instance, select the photo in Photos, press the Share icon⬆, select Mail, and then send yourself a message.

❖ On the other device, access the email to download any attachments.

Before receiving a file using Mail on a Mac, for instance, pick the email that contains the attachment and then select File > Save Attachments.

Depending on your email service provider and Internet service provider (ISP), there may be size restrictions on the files you transmit.

Use text communications for file transmission

Ensure that messaging is configured on your smartphone and computer before proceeding.

❖ Attach a file to an iPhone or computer message, and then transmit the communication to yourself.

To transmit a photo via your iPhone via Messages, for instance, pick the photo in Photos, press the Share icon⬆️, select Messages, and then send yourself a message.

❖ Open the message attachment and save it to the other device.

For instance, using Messages on a Mac for getting a photo, Control-click the photo's attachment and select Add to Photos.

Important: Standard data and text messaging rates may apply. Your carrier might impose size restrictions on attachments. When necessary, iPhone can compress photo and video attachments.

Utilize Airdrop for file transmission

On a Mac running OS X 10.10 or later, you may utilize AirDrop to transfer files between your Mac and iPhone. AirDrop transfers data using Bluetooth and Wi-Fi, and the devices have to be nearby. (Make certain Wi-Fi and Bluetooth are enabled on your Mac and iPhone.) Transfers are encrypted to ensure their security.

For the use of AirDrop, you have to have your Apple ID signed in on both the iPhone and Mac.

❖ Select an object on the device or computer.

❖ Tap or select the icon (such as Share⬆, AirDrop, or More options) that displays the app's sharing options.

   To transmit a photo from the iPhone using AirDrop, for instance, swipe the Share icon after selecting the photo in Photos.

❖ Select the other device by tapping or clicking the AirDrop icon ⊚ in the sharing menu.

Following an item has been delivered to your iPhone, you can locate it in the app to which you saved it or in the app that opened automatically. After an item has been sent to your Mac, you can locate it in the application where you saved it or in the Downloads folder.

CHAPTER TEN

HOW TO BACKUP AND RESTORE YOUR IPHONE

The iPhone can be backed up via iCloud or your computer. If you update your iPhone, you can transfer your data to the new device using its backup.

USING ICLOUD, BACK UP IPHONE

❖ To access iCloud Backup, navigate to Settings > [your name] > iCloud > iCloud Backup.
❖ Enable iCloud Backup.

When your iPhone is powered, secured, and connected to Wi-Fi, iCloud will automatically back it up every day.

On 5G-capable iPhone models, your carrier may provide a choice to back up your iPhone using the cellular network. Navigate to Settings > [your name] > iCloud > iCloud Backup and toggle Backup Over Cellular on or off.

❖ To create a backup manually, tap Back Up Now.

Select Settings > [your username] > iCloud > Control Account Storage > Backups to view your iCloud backups. Select a backup from the list that appears, then select Delete & Set Off Backup to delete it.

Note: If you enable iCloud syncing for an app or feature (in Settings > [your name] > iCloud > Show

All), its data is stored in iCloud. Because the data is automatically updated on all of your devices, it is not backed up to iCloud.

UTILIZE MAC FOR BACKUP

❖ Cable-connect your iPhone to your computer.
❖ In the Mac Finder's sidebar, select your iPhone.

For iPhone backups using the Finder, macOS 10.15 or later must be installed. Previous versions of macOS require iTunes for iPhone backups.

❖ Click General at the top of the Finder window.
❖ Select "Backup all of the information on your iPhone to this Mac."
❖ To encrypt and password-protect your backup data, select "Encrypt local backup."
❖ Click Restore Now.

Note: You can also attach your iPhone wirelessly to your computer if you configure synchronization over Wi-Fi.

IPHONE CAN BE BACKED UP USING A WINDOWS PC

❖ Cable-connect your iPhone to your computer.
❖ Click the iPhone icon near the upper left of the iTunes window on your PC's iTunes app.
❖ Click Overview.
❖ Click Backup Now (listed beneath Backups).
❖ Select "Encrypt local backup," enter a password, and then press Set Password to encrypt your backups.

To view the copies of backups stored on your machine, click Devices after selecting Edit > Preferences. There is a lock icon next to encrypted backups in the list of backups.

RESTORE ALL IPHONES FROM A BACKUP

You may restore information, settings, and applications from a backup to a brand-new or recently-deleted iPhone.

Important: Before proceeding, you must generate a duplicate of your iPhone. Refer to Backup iPhone.

Restoring from an iCloud backup

❖ Turn on a brand-new or recently wiped iPhone.
❖ Perform one of the subsequent:
  ✓ Select Set Up Manually, then select Restore from iCloud Backup, and then follow the instructions on-screen.
  ✓ If you have a different iPad, iPhone, or iPod touched with iOS 11, iPadOS 13, or a later version, you may utilize Quick Start to configure your new device automatically. Follow the on-screen instructions to securely replicate many of the settings, tastes, and iCloud keychains. The remainder of your data and content can then be restored to the newly purchased gadget from your iCloud backup.

  Alternatively, if both gadgets have iOS 12.4, iPadOS 13, or a later version, you can wirelessly transfer all of your data from your former device to your new device. Keep your devices close to one another and powered up until the migration is complete.

You must enter your Apple ID. Visit the site for recovering your Apple ID website if you have forgotten your Apple ID.

Recover iPhone from a backup on a computer

❖ Attach a new or recently wiped iPhone via USB to the computer holding your backup.
❖ Perform one of the subsequent:
  ✓ Macs running macOS 10.15 or later: Select your iPhone in the Finder sidebar, hit Trust, and then click "Restore from this backup."
  ✓ On the Mac (macOS 10.14 or earlier) or a Windows-based personal computer: select the icon resembling an iPhone in the upper left corner of the iTunes window, then select Summary, followed by Restore Backup.

Use the most recent version of iTunes.

❖ Select your backup from the drop-down menu, then select Continue.

Before restoring your data and settings, you must input the password if your backup is encrypted.

Erase iPhone

When you delete data, it disappears from iPhone apps but is not removed from iPhone storage. To permanently delete all content and preferences from your iPhone, you must erase (clean) it. Delete your iPhone before selling, trading in, or giving it away.

There are two methods for erasing an iPhone: using Settings on the iPhone itself, or connecting the iPhone to a computer via a USB cable and employing the Finder or iTunes. The simplest method is Settings. If you cannot access Settings, you must connect the iPhone to the computer using the Finder or iTunes.

Before you start

❖ If you intend to sell, trade-in, or give away your iPhone.
❖ To preserve your information and settings, restore your iPhone just before deleting it or when prompted to do so during the process. You may recover your data on an updated iPhone or iPad using the backup.
❖ Keep your iPhone passcode Apple ID password handy.

Erase using iPhone Settings

❖ From the menu, go to Preferences > General > Transfer or Reset iPhone.
❖ Perform one of the subsequent:
   ✓ Prepare your iPhone's content and settings for transfer: Tap Start, then adhere to the on-screen instructions. Continue to Settings > General > Transfer or Reset iPhone, then select Erase All Content and Settings when you are finished.

✓ Delete all data from your iPhone: Tap Clear Settings and Content.

Employ a computer to delete an iPhone

❖ You may delete your mobile device's information and preferences, restore it to its original state, and reinstall the most current version of iOS using a Macintosh or Windows PC.

❖ Using a USB or USB-C cable, link your iPhone to your computer. You may need an adapter as well.

❖ Activate your iPhone.

❖ Perform one of the subsequent:

✓ Macs running macOS 10.15 or later: Click the Finder icon in the Dock to launch a Finder window. Click the iPhone option in the Finder sidebar (below Locations).

✓ On a Mac (macOS 10.14 or previous) or a Windows PC: Ensure that you have the most recent version of iTunes select the iPhone icon in the upper left corner of iTunes, then select Summary, followed by Restore iPhone.

RESTORE THE IPHONE'S SETTINGS TO FACTORY DEFAULTS

You can reset settings to their factory defaults without losing your data.

If you want to preserve your settings, you must back up your iPhone before resetting it to factory settings. For instance, if restoring settings to their defaults does not resolve a problem, you may wish to reclaim previous settings from a backup.

❖ Navigate to Settings > General > Transfer or Reset > Reset on your iPhone.
❖ Select one option:
❖ Reset All Settings: All settings are withdrawn or reset to their default values, such as network settings, the keypad dictionary, geolocation settings, settings for privacy, and Apple Pay cards. No data or media are erased.
❖ Resetting network settings removes all network settings. Additionally, the device name in Settings > General > About is reset to "iPhone," and explicitly trusted certificates (such as those for websites) are changed to untrusted.

Additionally, data roaming may be disabled.

Recently utilized networks and VPN settings that were not installed by a setup profile or MDM (mobile device management) are removed when you reset network settings. The deactivation and reactivation of Wi-Fi results in the disconnection from any previously linked network. The settings for Wi-Fi and the option to prompt for joining networks are now activated.

Navigate to Settings to delete VPN configurations established by a configuration profile.> General > VPN & Device Management, pick the profile and then tap Remove Profile. This also deletes the profile's additional configurations and accounts.

To remove MDM-installed network settings, navigate to Settings > General > VPN & Device Management, pick the management, and then tap Remove Management. This also removes additional MDM settings and certificates.

❖ You add terms to the keypad dictionary by declining the suggestions the iPhone makes as you type. When you reset the keyboard dictionary, only the words you've added are removed.

❖ Reset Home Screen configuration: Returns the native applications' Home Screen configuration to its original state.

❖ Restore Location & Privacy: Restores the default location services as well as privacy settings.

CHAPTER ELEVEN

CAMERA APPLICATION

IOS CAMERA FUNDAMENTALS

Understanding how to utilize the Camera app on your iPhone, to compose your image, choose from options such as Photo, Cinematic, Video, Pano, and Portrait, and zoom in or out.

The camera is in the Photo mode, with the other modes listed below the viewfinder. The LED Flash, Camera Controls, and Live Photo buttons are displayed at the top of the screen. The option for the Picture and Video Viewer is located in the lower-left quadrant. The Take Picture button is located in the bottom center, while the Camera Selector Back-Facing button is located.

Open Camera

❖ To launch the Camera, perform any option below:

- Select Camera on the Home screen of the iPhone.
- Press and hold the Camera button 📷 on the Lock Screen of the iPhone.
- Tap the Camera icon 📷 after opening Control Center.

Siri: Say a thing like: "Open Camera."

Note: A green dot appears in the upper-right corner of the screen when the Camera is active for your safety. See Manage access to hardware capabilities.

To capture a photo, launch the Camera and then touch the Shutter button or the volume button.

Select among camera modes

Photo is the default mode displayed when you open Camera. Use the Photo mode to capture both still and moving images. Swipe the screen to the left or right to select one of the following camera modes:

- Video: Capture a video;
- Create a time-lapse video of motion over an extended period;
- Slo-mo: Record a video in slow motion.
- Take a panoramic photograph of a landscape or other scene;
- Apply a depth-of-field effect to your portrait photographs (on supported devices);
- Cinematic: Apply a depth-of-field effect to your videos (on models supported);
- Take photographs with a square aspect ratio.

❖ Select the Camera Controls icon , then select 4:3 to toggle between square, 4:3, and 16:9 aspect ratios on iPhone.

UTILIZE IPHONE CAMERA TOOLS TO ENHANCE IMAGES

You can use Camera tools to customize and enhance your image before taking it.

Adjust the focus and exposure of the camera

❖ The camera on an iPhone regulates the focal point and exposure before snapping a photo recognizes faces, and adjusts the exposure across numerous features. To change the instrument's focus and exposure manually, do the following:

❖ Open Camera.

❖ Tap the display to display the area of automatic focus and the exposure setting.

❖ Tap where you wish to relocate the focus.

❖ To adjust the exposure, drag the Adjust Exposure icon next to the area of focus up or down.

Continue to touch and hold the focus area until you see AE/AF Lock; tap the screen to unlock the settings.

On iPhone 11 and subsequent models, it is possible to precisely define and secure the exposure for forthcoming photos. Select the Camera Controls button , then the Exposure button, and then drag the exposure slider. The exposure is locked until the next time Camera is opened. To save the exposure control so that it is not reset when the Camera is opened, navigate to Settings > Camera > Preserve Settings and then enable Exposure Adjustment.

Switch the light on or off

Your iPhone camera is configured to use the flash automatically when necessary. To manually control the light before taking a photograph, perform the steps below:

- ❖ Tap the illumination icon ⚡ on iPhone XS, iPhone XR, and later models to enable or disable the automatic illumination. Tap the Camera Controls ⌃ icon, and then tap the Flash icon below the frame to select Auto, On, or Off ⚡.
- ❖ On iPhone X and prior models: Select Auto, On, or Off by tapping the Flash icon.

Take a picture using a filter

Apply a filter to impart a color effect to your photograph.

- ❖ Open the camera, select the Photo or Portrait mode, and then do one of the subsequent:
  - ✓ On iPhone XS, iPhone XR, and subsequent models: Tap the Camera Controls icon followed by the Filters icon ⊕.
  - ✓ Before iPhone X, tap the Filters icon ⬤ at the top of the display.

❖ Swipe the filters to the left or right below the viewer to evaluate them; select one to apply it.

In Photos, you can remove or alter a photo's filter.

Utilize preset

You can set a timer on your iPhone's camera to allow yourself time to position yourself for the picture.

To set a timer, launch Camera and then select one of the options below:

Press the Camera Controls switch⬆, tap the Timer button⏱, select 3s or 10s, and then tap the Shutter button to initiate the timer on iPhone XS, iPhone XR, and later.

Tap the Timer button⏱, select 3s or 10s, and then tap the Shutter button to initiate the timer on an iPhone X or earlier model.

Utilize a grid to align your photo

To display a grid on the camera's interface to help you align and compose your shots, navigate to Settings > Camera and enable Grid.

You may utilize the editing tools in the Photos application to further align photos and alter horizontal and vertical perspectives after taking a photo.

HOW TO TAKE LIVE PHOTOS

Utilize the Camera on the iPhone to take Live Photos. A Live Photo captures the audio from the moments just before and following the photo is taken. You snap a Live Photo just like you do a conventional photo.

❖ Open Camera.
❖ Ensure that the Camera mode has been set to Photo and that the Live Photo is activated.

When Live Photo is enabled, the Live Photo icon ◎ shows at the top of the display. A vertical line through the Live Photo icon indicates that the feature is disabled. Tap the icon to enable or disable Live Photo.

❖ To snap a Live Photo, touch the Shutter icon.
❖ Tap the photo icon at the bottom of your screen, then contact and hold the display to play the Live Photo.

UTILIZE PHOTOGRAPHIC STYLES ON THE IPHONE CAMERA

You may apply a Photographic Style to iPhone 15 designs to customize how the Camera captures images. Choose one of the preset styles—Rich Contrast, Warm, Vibrant, or Cool—and then modify the tone and temperature values to further customize it. Each time you take a photo in Photo mode, your settings are applied. In-camera changes and adjustments to Photographic Styles are possible.

Select a Photographic Technique

The camera is automatically set to Standard, a realistic and balanced approach. To apply a distinct Photographic Style, follow the steps below:

❖ Select the Camera Controls icon after launching the Camera application.

❖ To preview the various photographic styles, touch the Photographic Styles icon, then swipe to the left.

    ✓ Rich Contrast: Deeper shadows, more vibrant colors, and increased contrast produce a dramatic appearance.

    ✓ Wonderfully vibrant and vibrant hues create a natural yet spectacular appearance.

    ✓ Golden overtones produce a warming appearance.

    ✓ Blue undertones produce a colder appearance.

To modify a Photographic Design, touch the Tone as well as Warmth controls beneath the frame then drag the slider to the left or right to change the value. To reset the values, tap the Reset button ⟳ next to Photographic Styles.

❖ To apply a Photographic Style, select the Photographic Styles icon ▨ .

To modify a previously set Photographic Style, select the Photographic Styles On icon ▩ at the top of the display.

In Settings, you can also alter Photographic Styles: navigate to Options > Camera > Photographic Styles.

TAKE A SELF-PORTRAIT WITH YOUR IPHONE

❖ Open Camera.
❖ To transition to the front-facing camera, tap the Camera Chooser Back-Facing button or the Camera Chooser Back-Facing button.
❖ They must be held in front of you.
❖ Select the Shutter button or the volume button to capture an image or begin recording.

Go to Settings > Camera, then toggle Mirrors Front Camera (on iPhone XS, iPhone XR, as well as later) or Mirrors Front Photos (iPhone X and earlier) to take a selfie that captures the image when you see it in the front-facing camera frame, rather than in reverse.

CAPTURING ACTION PHOTOS WITH IPHONE'S BURST MODE

Use Camera's Burst mode to photograph a moving subject or capture multiple high-speed photographs so you have a variety of images to choose from. The rear and front-facing sensors both support Burst photography.

❖ Open Camera.
❖ Perform one of the subsequent:
   ✓ Swipe the Shutter icon to the left on, iPhone XR, and iPhone XS including subsequent devices.
   ✓ Hold down the Shutter button on the iPhone X and prior models.

   The counter displays the number of bullets taken.

❖ Raise your pointer to halt.
❖ To select the desired photos, tap the Burst thumbnail and then tap Select.

   Below the thumbnails, gray outlines indicate the suggested photos to retain.

❖ Tap the circle in the lower-right side of each image you wish to save as a separate image, and then tap Done.

Tap the thumbnail and then the erase icon 🗑 to erase the entire Burst.

Tip: You can also snap Burst photos by pressing and holding the volume up button. Turn on Use Volume Up for Burst in Settings > Camera

TAKE PANORAMIC IMAGES WITH THE IPHONE'S CAMERA

Use a Camera in Pano mode to capture a panoramic image of your environment.

❖ Choose Pano mode.
❖ Tap the shutter release switch.
❖ Slowly pan in the direction of the arrow, maintaining its position on the center line.
❖ To conclude, press the Shutter icon once more.

To pan in the opposite direction, tap the arrow. To pan vertically, orient the iPhone in landscape mode. Additionally, you can reverse the orientation of a vertical pan.

TAKE MACRO PHOTOGRAPHS AND RECORDINGS

It is possible to take macro images and Live Photos, as well as macro slow-motion and time-lapse recordings.

Take macro photographs or films

Launch the camera, then select either the photo or video mode.

Get as near to the subject as 2 centimeters will allow.
Automatically, the camera will transition to Ultra Wide mode.

❖ Tap the Shutter button to capture a photo, and the Record button to begin and end video recording.

Take a macro time-lapse or slow-motion video

❖ Launch the camera, then select the Slow Motion or Time-lapse mode.
❖ Tap.5x to transition to Ultra Wide mode, then approach the subject.
❖ Tap the Record icon to initiate and terminate recording.

Manage automatic macro selection

You may regulate when the camera instantly transitions to the Ultra Wide lens for macro photography and videography.

- ❖ Navigate to Settings > Camera and enable Macro Control.
- ❖ Open the camera, then approach the subject.
- ❖ When the subject is within the macro range, the Macro icon appears on the screen.
- ❖ Tap the Macro icon to disable the automatic toggling of macros.
- ❖ If the image or video becomes indistinct, you can swipe backward or tap.5x to access the Ultra Wide camera mode.
- ❖ To restore automatic macro toggling, tap the Macro icon.

Employ the Camera within macro range, and automatic macro switching is enabled again. Go to Settings > Camera > Preserve Settings and enable Macro Control if you want to preserve your Macro Control setting between camera sessions.

HOW TO CAPTURE PORTRAIT MODE IMAGES

On Portrait mode-enabled Camera models, you can employ a depth-of-field effect that maintains your subject (humans, pets, objects, etc.) in focus while blurring the foreground and background. You can apply and modify various lighting effects to Portrait mode pictures, and with the iPhone X and subsequent models, you can even capture a portrait selfie.

Capture an image in Portrait mode

Portrait mode photos can be enhanced with studio-quality illumination effects.

The camera interface is in Portrait mode; the subject is distinct while the background is obscured in the viewfinder. The dial to select Portrait lighting effects is open and Studio Light is selected at the bottom of the frame. The Flash button, Camera Controls button, and Portrait illumination intensity and depth control buttons are located in the upper left and right corners of the screen, respectively. At the bottom of the display are the Picture and Video Viewer switch, the Take Photo button, and the Photo and Video Chooser Back-Facing button, from left to right.

❖ Launch the camera and select Portrait mode.
❖ Follow the on-screen instructions to position your subject within the yellow portrait area.
❖ To select a lighting effect, drag the Portrait Lighting slider:

Natural Light: The visage is in fine focus while the background is out of focus.

Studio Light: The appearance is well-illuminated, and the photograph has an overall neat appearance.

There are dramatic shadows and highlights and lowlights on the visage.

The face is spot-lit against a deep black backdrop with stage lighting.

Similar to Stage Light, but with a black-and-white photograph.

High-Key Light Mono: Produces a grayscale subject against a white background (available on iPhone XS, iPhone XR, and subsequent models).

❖ Tap the Shutter icon to capture an image.

If you don't like the Portrait mode effect after taking a photo in Portrait mode, you can eradicate it. Open the photo in the Photos app, select Edit, and then touch Portrait to enable or disable the effect.

Note: Stage Light, Stage Lighting Mono, and High-Key Light Mono are only accessible when using the front camera on the iPhone XR.

Change Depth Control settings in Portrait mode

Use the Depth Control toggle on iPhone XS, iPhone XR, and later models to adjust the amount of background haze in Portrait mode photographs.

❖ Initiate the Camera app, select Portrait mode, and then frame your subject.

❖ Select the Depth Adjustment icon in the screen's upper-right quadrant.

❖ The Depth Control adjuster is located underneath the frame.

❖ To adjust the effect, drag the slider to the right or left.

❖ Tap the Shutter icon to capture an image.

After taking a photo in portrait orientation, you can further alter the background haze effect using the Depth Control slider in Photos.

HOW TO TAKE APPLE PRORAW PICTURES

The Camera app on iPhone 15 Pro Max supports Apple ProRAW. Apple ProRAW blends the data of a standard RAW format with iPhone image processing to provide additional creative control over the exposure, hue, and white balance adjustments.

Apple ProRAW is supported by every camera, including the front-facing camera. Apple ProRAW is incompatible with Portrait mode.

Configure Apple ProRAW

To configure Apple ProRAW on models that support it, navigate to Settings > Camera > Formats, then enable Apple ProRAW.

Note that Apple ProRAW images retain more image data, leading to larger file sizes.

Capture a picture using the Apple ProRAW

❖ Open the Camera, then touch the Raw Off icon to activate ProRAW.
❖ Make your move

As you shot, you can alternate using the Raw On and Raw Off buttons to activate and deactivate ProRAW.

To preserve your ProRAW settings, navigate to Preferences > Camera > Preserve Settings and activate Apple ProRAW.

Change Apple ProRAW image quality

iPhone 15 Pro Max can capture 12 MP and 48 MP ProRAW images.

❖ Go to Configuration > Camera > Formats.
❖ Turn on Apple ProRAW (green is on), then select either 12 MP or 48 MP from the ProRAW Resolution menu.

HOW TO TAKE PHOTOS IN NIGHT MODE

On supported models, Camera's Night mode can be utilized to capture additional information and enhance low-light images. In Night mode, the duration of the exposure is determined automatically; however, you can play with the manual controls.

Use a tripod to capture more comprehensive Night mode images.

Night mode is accessible on the iPhone variants and cameras listed below:

- ❖ Open Camera. In low-light conditions, Night mode automatically activates.
- ❖ Select the Night mode icon at the highest point of the screen to enable or disable Night mode.
- ❖ To begin playing with Night mode, touch the Camera Controls icon, tap the Night mode button in the bottom array of options, and then use the slider to select between Auto and Max durations. Auto determines the exposure duration

automatically, while Max employs the largest exposure time. The settings you select are retained for future Night mode photos.

Tap the Shutter icon and hold the camera steady to snap a picture.

If your iPhone senses motion during capture, crosshairs will appear in the frame; aligning the crosshairs will help you reduce motion and enhance the image.

Tap the halt icon below the slider to halt capturing a Night mode photo mid-capture.

VIDEO RECORDINGS

Use the iPhone's Camera to record videos and QuickTake videos.

Note: A greenish dot shows up on the upper-right side of the display when the Camera is active to protect your privacy.

Record a video

❖ Launch the camera and select Video mode.
❖ To begin recording, tap the Record button or touch either volume control. While recording, the following can be done:
  ✓ Use the white Shutter icon to capture a still image.
  ✓ Simply pinch the display to expand in and out.
  ✓ Touch and hold 1x and then drag the slider to the left for a more precise magnification on models with Dual and Triple camera systems.

❖ To cease recording, hit the Record button or touch either volume control.

Video is recorded at thirty frames per second, or fps for short, by default. Setup > the camera > Begin Video, you can change the frame rate and video resolution depending on your model. Higher frame rates and resolutions lead to larger video file sizes.

Employ Action mode

Action mode provides enhanced stabilization while recording in Video mode on iPhone 15 models. To enable Action Mode, tap the Action Mode Off button at the top of the screen, and to disable it, tap the Action Mode On icon.

Action mode performs optimally in strong light. To use Action Mode in low-light conditions, Go to Preferences, Camera, Recording Video, and turn on Action Mode. Dim the Light. The greatest capture resolution in action mode is 2,8K.

Create a QuickTake recording

On iPhone XS, iPhone XR, and subsequent models, it is possible to record QuickTake videos. A QuickTake video is a recording made in Photo mode. While recording a QuickTake video, you can secure the Record button and continue to capture still images.

Touch and hold the Shutter button while the Camera is in Photo mode to begin recording a QuickTake video.

❖ To record hands-free, move the Shutter button to the right and release it over the lock.

❖ Below the frame are the Record and Shutter controls; press the Shutter button to take a still photo while recording.

   ✓ To focus on your subject, swipe up, or if you are recording hands-free, press out on the screen.

   ✓ To cease recording, tap the Record icon.

To begin recording a QuickTake video in the Photo mode, press and hold the volume up or volume down button.

Tap the thumbnail to open the QuickTake movie in the Photos app.

Recording a slow-motion video

When recording a video in slow-motion mode, the video is recorded normally and the slow-motion effect is only visible when you play the video back. Additionally, you can alter the footage so that the slow-motion action begins and ends at a particular time.

❖ Launch Camera, then select the Slow-motion mode.

❖ To begin recording, tap the Record button or touch either volume control.

❖ While recording, you can touch the Shutter icon to capture a still image.

❖ To cease recording, tap the Record button or touch either volume control.

To play a portion of the video in slow motion and the remainder at normal speed, touch the video thumbnail and then tap Edit. Use the vertical bars beneath the frame viewer to define the segment you wish to play in slow motion.

You can alter the slow-motion frame rate and resolution based on your model. To modify the parameters for slow-motion recording, navigate to parameters > Camera > Record Slo-mo.

Recording a time-lapse video

Capture footage at predetermined intervals to produce a time-lapse video of an event, such as the sun setting or traffic moving.

❖ Launch Camera and then select the Time-lapse mode.
❖ Position the iPhone where you wish to capture a moving scene.
❖ To begin recording, touch the Record icon; to end recording, tap it again.

Tip: For iPhone models 12 and later, use a tripod to record time-lapse videos in low-light conditions with greater clarity and luminosity.

Change the iPhone camera's video recording parameters

By default, the Camera records video at 30 frames per second (fps). Depending on the iPhone model, different frame rates and video resolutions are available. Higher frame rates and resolutions lead to larger video file sizes.

Additionally, you can use fast toggles to alter video resolution and frame rate directly on the camera's display.

To fast alter the resolution of videos and frame rate, use toggles

In Video mode, utilize the rapid switches at the highest point of the screen to change the acceptable video size and frame rate on the iPhone.

Tap the rapid toggles in the upper-right quadrant of the iPhone XS, XR, and later models to choose between HD or 4K recording and 24, 25, 30, or 60 frames per second in Video mode.

To enable fast toggles on iPhone X and earlier models, navigate to Settings > Camera > Record Video and enable Video Format Control.

On iPhone 15 models, Cinematic mode provides fast toggles for switching between HD or 4K and 24, 25, or 30 frames per second.

Adjust Auto FPS parameters

By automatically lowering the frame rate to 24 fps in low-light situations, iPhone XS, iPhone XR, and later models can enhance video quality.

❖ Navigate to Settings > Camera > Record Video

❖ Tap Auto FPS and select the appropriate frame rate

Note: Auto FPS can be applied to only 30-fps video or it can be applied to both 30- and 60-fps videos.

On and off switch for stereo recording

On iPhone XS, iPhone XR, and later models, stereo sound is produced by multiple microphones. To disable stereo recording, navigate to Settings > Camera and disable Record Stereo Sound.

Turn off and on HDR video

iPhone 15 models record video in HDR and can share HDR videos with iPadOS 13.4, iOS 13.4, macOS 10.15, or subsequent releases; other devices receive an SDR rendition of the same video. To disable HDR recording, navigate to Settings > Camera > Record Video and disable HDR Video.

Turn Camera Lock on and off

The Lock Camera setting on the iPhone 15 prevents the automatic toggling between cameras during video recording. This is by default disabled.

To enable Lock Camera navigate to Settings > Camera > Record Video, and then enable Lock Camera.

Turn off and on Enhanced stabilization

Enhanced Stabilization zooms in slightly on iPhone 15 models to enhance stabilization when filming in

Video mode and Cinematic mode. By default, Enhanced Stabilization is enabled.

To disable **Enhanced Stabilization** navigate to Settings > Camera > Capture Video and disable Enhanced Stabilization.

HOW TO SHARE, VIEW, AND PRINT PHOTOS

All images and videos captured with the Camera are preserved in the Photos folder. With iCloud Photos enabled, all new videos and pictures are immediately uploaded and made accessible in Photos on all iCloud-enabled devices (iOS 8.1, iPadOS 13, or later).

Note: If Location Services is enabled in Settings > Privacy & Security > Places Services, pictures, and videos are tagged with location information that apps and photo-sharing websites can access.

View your images

❖ Select the thumbnail picture in the lower-left corner after launching Camera.
❖ Slide left or right to view your most recent photos.
❖ Tap the display to show or conceal the controls.
❖ Select All Photos to view all of your Photos-stored photos and videos.

Print and share your photographs

❖ In the photo viewer, select the Share icon .
❖ Chose an option that includes AirDrop, Mail, or Messages to share your photo.

❖ Swipe up and select Print from the list of actions to print your photo.

Upload images and maintain their consistency across devices

Using iCloud Photos, you can upload pictures and videos from your iPhone to iCloud followed by accessing them on other Apple-identified devices. If you want to keep your photos up-to-date across multiple devices or free up capacity on your iPhone, iCloud Photos is beneficial. Go to Settings > Photos to enable iCloud Photos.

CHAPTER TWELVE

HOW TO MAKE CALLS WITH AN IPHONE

To initiate a call in the Phone app , input the amount on the keypad, tap a recent or favored call, or select a contact.

Dial a number

Siri: Say "call" or "dial" and then the number. Speak each digit individually, such as "four one five, five five five..." In the United States, the 800 area code is referred to as "eight hundred."

Alternatively, do the following:

❖ Tap Keypad.

❖ Perform any of the subsequent:
- ✓ Apply a different line: Tap the line at the top of Dual SIM models, then select a line.
- ✓ Enter the number via the numeric keypad: If you make an error, press the Delete key ❌..
- ✓ Dial the previous number: Press the Call button 📞 to view the most recent number you dialed, and then press the Call button 📞 again to dial that number.
- ✓ Copy a number and then paste it: Select the cell phone number field atop the keypad, followed by Paste.
- ✓ Insert a two-second pause: Press and hold the stars (*) key until you see a comma.
- ✓ Enter a firm suspend (to halt dialing until the Dial button is pressed): Hold down the pounds (#) key until you see a semicolon.
- ✓ For international conversations, type "+" Hold the "o" key until the "+" symbol appears.

❖ Touch the contact icon 📞 to initiate contact.

Tap the terminate Call icon ⬤. to terminate a call.

Call your loved ones

❖ Tap Favorites, then select a contact to call.

On Dual SIM models, the iPhone selects the line for a call in the next order:

- ✓ If set, the preferred phone number for this contact.
- ✓ The number of the last call made from or to this contact.
- ✓ The standard vocal connection
- ❖ Use one of the options below for handling your Favorites list:
  - ✓ Add a favorite: Tap the Add icon before selecting a contact.
  - ✓ Reorganize or delete favorites: Tap Edit.

Redial or answer a recent contact

Siri: Say "Redial that number" or "Return my last call."

Moreover, apply the options below:

- ❖ Tap Recents, then select a contact to call.
- ❖ To obtain additional information about an incoming call and the recipient, select the More Info icon ⓘ .

A scarlet badge displays the amount of ignored contacts.

Dial a number on your contact directory

Siri: Say something such as, "Call Mike's mobile."

Alternatively, do the following:

- ❖ To access Contacts in the Phone app, select Contacts.
- ❖ Tap the contact, followed by the desired phone number.

On Dual SIM models, the standard voice line is used unless a preferred voice line has been configured for the contact.

HOW TO MAKE CALLS ON WI-FI WITH IPHONE

Use Wi-Fi Calling when your iPhone has a weak cellular signal to make and get calls over a Wi-Fi network.

- ❖ On your iOS device, navigate to Settings > Cellular.
- ❖ If your iPhone supports Dual SIM, select a line below SIMs.
- ❖ Tap Wi-Fi Calling and activate Wi-Fi Calling on This iPhone.
- ❖ Enter your address or validate it for emergency services.

When Wi-Fi Calling is enabled, "Wi-Fi" appears in the status bar after your carrier's name and all of your calls are routed through Wi-Fi.

MODIFY YOUR OUTGOING CALL CONFIGURATION

- ❖ Navigate to Settings > Phone.
- ❖ Perform any of the subsequent:

✓ Bring on Display Caller ID: (GSM) My Number displays your phone number. FaceTime conversations display your phone number even if caller ID is disabled.
✓ Enable Dial Assist when making international calls: (GSM) While Dial Assist is activated; iPhone applies the correct foreign or local name when calling contacts and preferences.